G000114448

EW SOUTH WALES

Art Gallery of New South Wales

HANDBOOK

The *Art Gallery of New South Wales Handbook*
has been produced with funds provided by the
Art Gallery Society of New South Wales

Art Gallery
of New South Wales
HANDBOOK

First published in 1988
by The Trustees;
Art Gallery of New South Wales,
Art Gallery Road, Domain,
Sydney, New South Wales,
Australia 2000
Telephone (02) 225 1700

Copyright © The Trustees
ISBN 0 7305 4591 1

Compiler	Jacqueline Menzies
Editor	Annabel Davie, Fine Arts Press Pty Ltd, Sydney
Design & Production	Janet Gough, Fine Arts Press Pty Ltd, Sydney
Photography	Kerry Dundas and Ray Woodbury
Typesetting	In Baskerville by D.G.D. Pty Ltd, Sydney
Artwork	Robson Bookcraft Pty Ltd, Sydney
Printer	Pyung Hwa Dang Printing Company, Korea

Contents

Introduction

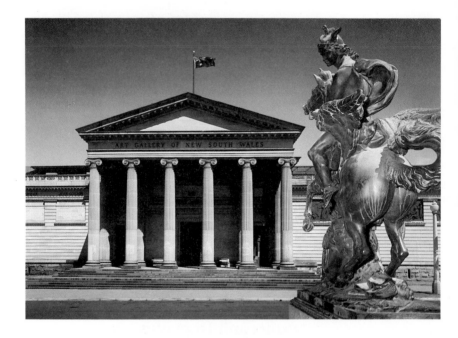

The Roman-style sandstone entrance façade designed by W. L. Vernon, and completed in 1909. In the right foreground is the nineteenth century bronze sculpture *Mercury* after a marble original by Antoine Coyzevox (French, 1640-1720).

Behind the imposing classical façade of W. L. Vernon's grand design for the Art Gallery of New South Wales lie, as expected, some of the finest achievements in the history of Australian art, some inspiring moments in the history of art from other parts of the world, and indeed some architectural surprises. A first time visitor to the Art Gallery of New South Wales may well be struck, after passing through the imposing nineteenth-century Vernon classic portico and elegant foyer, by the unqualified intrusion of the new wing which almost dramatically confronts the viewer through the classical arches of the vestibule. It is a bold statement, which in essence characterizes the happy but uncompromising blend of old and new that is such a feature of this Gallery.

The Art Gallery of New South Wales was formally established in 1874 out of the New South Wales Academy of Art. Fortunately the Ministry in charge of Education, upon seeking the advice of the Academy as to how funds should best be spent, concluded 'the money be put in the hands of Trustees who should appoint the Committee of Selection in London, the Trustees to have liberty to invest some portion of the money in the colony should it be deemed advisable'. From such small beginnings pictures were bought, principally in London, and the foundations of a collection were formed. Some two years later in 1876, the doors of the Academy were opened to the public on two days a week and the pictures put on view. Among these earliest purchases are some of the Gallery's outstanding works, for example Ford Madox Brown's *Chaucer at the Court of Edward III,* purchased in 1876, and Edward Poynter's *The visit of the Queen of Sheba to Solomon,* purchased in 1892, which provide the Gallery with a particular strength in British Victorian painting. At that time there was perhaps too strong an emphasis on 'contemporary' British art, although Australian works were acquired from the outset. Such an emphasis did, however, divert attention

Façade by W. L. Vernon with Captain Cook Bicentennial wing designed by Andrew Andersons, 1972.

away from other European traditions and the repercussions of that policy are felt today. It was not until the 1920s that non-British and Australian art was seriously sought and acquired by the Gallery, for example among the earliest French acquisitions are Fantin-Latour's *Flowers and fruit*, bought in 1923, and Camille Pissarro's *Peasants' houses, Eragny*, bought in 1935.

The collections are now broadly displayed according to curatorial responsibility under the Departments for Australian Art, European Art, Contemporary Art, Asian Art, Prints and Drawings and Photography. This introductory guide follows that discipline. In addition the Gallery maintains a collection of Aboriginal and Melanesian art, with its own galleries, which continues to expand. Such a guide cannot claim to be comprehensive, and indeed it is not; it seeks to provide the visitor with a general outline of the Gallery's collections and in doing so to highlight works that can to some extent characterize the quality and scope of those collections.

The publication of this guide coincides with the opening of the new extension to the Gallery. These additions provide us with the means to yet further develop and expand our services to the public, and of course to display a greater proportion of the permanent collections. Above all these new extensions give recognition to the more specialized display requirements of certain aspects of the collection; for example the outdoor sculpture garden on the roof, the specially designed and fitted gallery for Asian art and the spacious partially naturally lit rooms for contemporary art.

I trust this guide will enable visitors to derive greater benefit from our rich and developing collections and to enjoy the facilities of our now much enlarged building. It is my firm belief that art galleries and museums should, above all, be places of pleasure and enjoyment, interest and stimulus, even perhaps a little contention, and I hope we succeed, and will continue to succeed, in achieving such aspirations.

Edmund Capon, Director
April 1988.

History

The history of the Gallery began in 1871 with the formation of the parent institution, the New South Wales Academy of Art, following a public meeting on 24 April in that year convened by Edward Reeve, Curator of the University of Sydney's Nicholson Museum, and a teacher and journalist.

The Academy organized exhibitions between 1872 and 1877, and from 1875 it rented a building for lectures and classes in painting and sculpture, and for housing the first parts of its collection.

In 1874 five Trustees were appointed to administer a vote of £500 from the New South Wales Government 'towards the formation of a Gallery of Art'. This grant came from the Education Department of the Government, and the Gallery Trustees continued to be responsible to the Minister for Education until 1971.

From 1880, the Art Gallery of New South Wales began to be known by its present name. This lasted until 1883 when its name was changed to National Art Gallery of New South Wales. The Gallery was given a building to house its art collection and E. L. Montefiore, a founder Trustee and President of the Trustees from 1889, was appointed the first Director

The Fine Arts Annexe, Sydney International Exhibition 1879, with the Garden Palace beyond.

From a wood-engraving in the *Official Record of the International Exhibition.*

(The Gallery's home from 1880 to 1885).

Artist's rendering of W. L. Vernon's façade.

in 1892; he unfortunately died two years later and another Director was not appointed until 1912.

In the last year of the century, 1899, the Gallery was incorporated under a New South Wales Act of Parliament, 'The Library and Art Gallery Act', which established a Board of thirteen Trustees. This Act remained substantially unchanged until 1958 when a new Act of Parliament, the Art Gallery of New South Wales Act 1958, was passed. The Act removed the word 'National' from the Art Gallery's name and altered the method of appointment of the Trustees. In future the term of office was to be four years and not for life as in the past.

In 1971 the Art Gallery was transferred from the Department of Education to the newly formed Department of Cultural Activities. In 1975 this Department was re-structured to become the Department of Culture, Sport and Recreation; in 1976 Culture was incorporated into the Premier's Department. From 1986 the Gallery became part of a separate Ministry of the Arts.

The History of the Building

From 1876 the New South Wales Academy of Art rented a former dancing studio in Elizabeth Street to display the first acquisitions of the Gallery together with some loan material. It was available for public viewing on two afternoons a week, at first Fridays and Saturdays, and later Wednesdays and Saturdays from noon to 4 pm.

In July 1880 the Elizabeth Street premises were closed

and transferred to a building in the Botanic Gardens which re-opened on the 22 September 1880 as the Art Gallery of New South Wales. From that time on the Gallery was open daily to the public.

The present site in the Domain was opened in December 1885 in a building designed by an architect in private practice, John Horbury Hunt. Hunt's building cost £11,000 and was fireproof, weatherproof and well lit from above via a saw-tooth roof. There was much adverse comment about the structure which was stark and windowless and made of bare brick. It was often referred to as the 'art barn' or 'wool store'. However it was always considered only as a temporary expedient.

Horbury Hunt was dismissed by the Trustees in 1895 and W. L. Vernon, the New South Wales Colonial Architect, was invited to submit a design. Vernon's design is the basis of the present façade and the southern picture galleries. Two picture galleries to Vernon's design were opened in 1897 — today one of these galleries houses European Art and the other Australian Art. They are easily distinguished from later additions by the yellower timber in their parquet floor; later rooms contain much redder timber. One of these galleries replaced one of the three southern galleries built by Hunt; in 1899 two more picture galleries were opened, replacing Hunt's two remaining southern galleries. (The three matching northern galleries built by Hunt survived until 1969 when they were demolished to make way for the Captain Cook Bicentenary wing.)

In 1901, to the south of the four southern galleries, a long gallery was opened as a watercolour gallery and at each end of it a small domed room for statues. Nineteenth-century European art is now found in this gallery.

By 1902 Vernon's great masterpiece, the grand oval lobby, was completed together with the portico.

After 1909 nothing more was built from Vernon's original design. His plan was to include a series of

The Gallery as it was until 1969 showing J. Horbury Hunt's original structure at the back and the northern end of W. L. Vernon's façade.

large bronze reliefs, set in panels, on the outer walls. Only four of these six panels were ever completed; the six corresponding panels to the north of the portico remain empty, as do those on the southern and eastern façades. The four existing panels are arranged in chronological order of their civilizations: Assyria, Egypt, Greece and Rome.

The two large equestrian bronzes *The offerings of peace* and *The offerings of war*, which stand to either side of the portico, were not in the original Vernon design but were installed in 1926 in positions decided by the Trustee Sir John Sulman.

Across the road from the portico two smaller equestrian bronzes *Fame* and *Mercury* by Antoine Coyzevox (French, 1640-1720), were installed in 1964 by the Council of the City of Sydney.

By the late 1960s the buildings had become run down and it was decided by the New South Wales Government that a rebuilding of much of the site should form part of the Captain Cook Bicentenary celebrations. An appeal was launched to attract public funds that would match the Government's contribution.

The architect chosen was Andrew Andersons, and it was his task to complete the new structure for 1972. It was finally decided to demolish the remaining parts of the Horbury Hunt temporary structure of 1885 and to complete the original ground plan of that time. Almost all of the Vernon structure was to be restored. The Gallery reopened in 1972 with its exhibition space doubled.

The second new large extension to the Gallery was opened in 1988 to the east of the existing structure. The extension was one of numerous Bicentennial projects undertaken by the State Government to commemorate two hundred years of white settlement in Australia. This extension was also the responsibility of Andrew Andersons and with the opening of this new wing the Gallery doubled its size. The new eastern extension expanded the display space for the permanent collections and includes special galleries for the Gallery's own holdings of Asian art, prints and drawings and photography. This new extension also accommodates, in addition to exhibition space, a new and enlarged home for the Art Gallery Society, the 350 seat Domain Theatre, a coffee-bar/café, and a rooftop sculpture garden.

(This 'History of the Gallery' has been adapted and condensed from a more detailed history by Daniel Thomas to be found in *ART and Australia*, Volume 10 Number 1, July 1972).

Australian

W. C. PIGUENIT
Australian 1836-1914
Mount Olympus, Lake St
Clair, Tasmania 1875
oil on canvas
69 x 107cm
Gift of subscribers 1875

The strength of the collections of the Art Gallery of New South Wales begins with its holdings of late nineteenth-century Australian art, due largely to a tradition begun in 1875 of acquiring local contemporary paintings. One of the first decisions made by the Trustees when charged with the administration of the vote of 500 pounds was to commission a watercolour from the English-born Conrad Martens (1801-78), then the most respected senior artist in the colony. Martens delivered his completed *Apsley Falls*, 1874, to the New South Wales Academy of Art where it was displayed at the Academy's fourth annual exhibition in 1875. This exhibition included a number of paintings by the Tasmanian-born W. C. Piguenit (1836-1914) whose *Mount Olympus, Lake St. Clair, Tasmania,* 1875, (illus.) inspired a group of citizens to subscribe towards its purchase and present it to the 'proposed Gallery'.

The initiative of the first Trustees in recognizing living Australian artists was thus matched at once by a public gesture,' and although the larger proportion of that founding government grant went towards purchasing English watercolours, an important

JOHN GLOVER
Australian 1767-1849
Natives on the Ouse River, Van
Diemen's Land 1838
oil on canvas
78.5 x 115.6cm
Purchased with the assistance
of the Bain family 1985

precedent had been established in the acquisition of
these first two Australian works of art for the Gallery.

It was only much later in the twentieth century that
the Gallery began to acquire Australian art before 1875
with any kind of conscious scholarly purpose.
Consequently its colonial holdings are relatively small
compared with those of its sister institution across the
Domain, the State Library of New South Wales, and
with other public art museums in Australia.

Nevertheless the displays of colonial Australian art
include some of the most important works in the
Australian collection. Of particular note are *My last*

view of Italy, looking from the Alps over Juza painted
by John Glover (1767-1849) in Tasmania in 1835; and
his *Natives on the Ouse River, Van Diemen's Land,*
1838, (illus.) a poignant portrayal of the doomed race
of Tasmanian Aborigines; *Bush landscape with
waterfall and an Aborigine stalking native animals,
New South Wales,* 1860s, by John Skinner Prout (1806-
76); and *Waterfall, Strath Creek,* 1862, (illus.) by Eugene
von Guérard (1811-1901). Nearby are a number of
interesting figurative and portrait paintings including
works by Maurice Felton (1803-42), Marshall Claxton
(1813–81), Richard Noble (*c.*1812-?), Nicholas Chevalier

EUGENE VON GUÉRARD
Australian 1811-1901
Waterfall, Strath Creek (1862)
oil on canvas
83.2 x 65.7cm
Purchased 1967

(1828-1902) and Thomas Woolner (1825-92).

The potential deterioration from exposure to light prevents works from the Gallery's fine collection of colonial watercolours from being displayed for more than a few weeks annually, but particularly worthy of note are *The Gigantic Lyllie of New South Wales*, 1810, by John Lewin (1770-1819), *View of the Heads, Port Jackson*, 1853, (illus.) by Conrad Martens, and *Man with horse and cart*, 1872, by Abram Louis Buvelot (1814-88).

The division between the art of the colonial period before 1885 and that of the Australian impressionist school of the late 1880s and 1890s is not as sharp as might seem at first glance. Paintings which may be referred to as late colonial in mood were being produced in Australian art well after the impressionists had embarked upon their new vision of Antipodean light and life.

This style was influenced to some extent by photography, and is typified in paintings that are dark-toned, large in scale, and allied with a strong sense of academic finish. *A billabong of the Goulburn*, 1884, by H. J. Johnstone (1835-1907), *Sydney from the North Shore*, 1888, by C. H. Hunt (1857-1938) and W. G. Piguenit's *The upper Nepean*, 1888, and the *The flood*

CONRAD MARTENS
Australian 1801-1878
View of the Heads, Port
Jackson 1853
watercolour, gouache on paper
54.2 x 76.4cm
Purchased with assistance from
Overseas Containers Australia
Ltd 1986

CHARLES CONDER
Australian 1868-1909
Departure of the Orient —
Circular Quay 1888
oil on canvas
45.1 x 50.1cm
Purchased 1888

on the Darling, 1890, evoke the sense of the awe with
which most Europeans related to the Australian
landscape from the earliest colonial period. Piguenit
especially, continued to paint in this romantic vein
into the early years of the twentieth century.

In the large central court of the old wing the first
substantial strength of the Australian collections,
paintings of the so-called Heidelberg School, or
Australian Impressionism, are displayed. It is a notable
fact that the acquisition dates of many 'icons' of the
Australian collection are very close to, if not the same
as, the year in which they were painted. Housed in
the large and elegant central court of the old wing
are *Departure of the S.S. Orient-Circular Quay*, 1888,
(illus.) by Charles Conder (1868-1909), painted and
purchased in 1888, *'Fire's on', (Lapstone Tunnel)*, 1891,
(illus.) by Arthur Streeton (1867-1943), purchased in

1893, *Shearing at Newstead (The Golden Fleece),* (illus.) by Tom Roberts (1856-1931), painted and purchased in 1894, *A summer evening* by David Davies. (1864-1939), painted and purchased in 1896, *On the wallaby track,* 1895, (illus.) by Frederick McCubbin (1855-1917), purchased in 1897, and *The storm,* 1896, by Walter Withers (1854-1914), purchased in 1897, to name a few. They signify not only great moments in the history of Australian art, but also astute acts of recognition by the Gallery in forming its Australian collections.

Of all the Australian works displayed in the old courts, however, the paintings which make the greatest impact in terms of sheer physical scale and ambitious composition are those of two expatriates who are among the most gifted Australian painters of the human figure, Rupert Bunny (1864-1947) and George Lambert (1873-1930). Bunny, who spent most of his working life in France, dominates the end wall of the central court with his magnificently sumptuous *A*

*summer morning, c.*1908, (illus.) and *Summer time, c.*1907; and Lambert nearby with his heroic *Across the black soil plains,* 1899, and *Holiday in Essex,* 1910, (illus.). In fact Bunny's great centrepiece *Summer time* may, by its vast sensuous orchestration of figures, momentarily distract the visitor's attention from the presence of a number of other fine paintings hanging nearby: *The ferry, c.*1910-11, (illus.) by another expatriate, Emanuel Phillips Fox (1865-1915), and *The sisters,* 1904, (illus.) by Hugh Ramsay (1877-1906); some small non-Australian subjects by Charles Conder and David Davies; and the decorative masterpiece *Pan,* 1889, by Sydney Long (1871-1955) in which the artist's blending of mythological fantasy with the Australian bush found its highest expression. A number of good examples of nineteenth- and early twentieth-century

GEORGE W. LAMBERT
Australian 1873-1930
Holiday in Essex 1910
oil on canvas
183.8 x 230.6cm
Purchased with assistance from
the Art Gallery Society of New
South Wales and the Marshall
Bequest Fund 1981

HUGH RAMSAY
Australian 1877-1906
The sisters 1904
oil on canvas
125.7 x 144.8cm
Purchased 1921

sculpture including works by Benjamin Law (1807-90), Bertram Mackennal (1863-1931), and Charles Web Gilbert (1867-1925) are displayed in the same court.

The twentieth-century Australian collection is housed in the ground floor gallery of the Captain Cook wing of the Gallery, and begins with the modern era. Ideas about modern art took a long time to take root in Australia. But it may be seen that in the paint handling and rhythmical compositions typical of the paintings of a new generation of artists — Roland Wakelin (1887-1971) in his *Down the hills to Berry's Bay*, 1916, (illus.) and *Synchromy in orange major*,

RUPERT BUNNY
Australian 1864-1947
A summer morning (*c.*1908)
oil on canvas
223 x 180.3cm
Purchased 1911

ROLAND WAKELIN
Australian 1887-1971
Down the hills to Berry's
Bay 1916
oil on canvas on hardboard
45.7 x 35.5cm
Purchased 1967

1919, Grace Cossington Smith (1892–1984) in her *The sock knitter*, 1915, and *Rushing*, *c*.1923, — Post-Impressionism from England and Europe was being taken seriously in Sydney by a small and isolated group of artists.

Even the conservative landscapist Elioth Gruner (1882-1939), who looked to Streeton for his early inspiration, became an exponent of the brushwork that was part of the first modern art in Sydney. His best paintings of the period are much loved by visitors who revere the pastoral landscape tradition promoted by Streeton. But these works, and the early paintings by Wakelin, reflect as much as anything else the influence of an exhibition of paintings by Emanuel Phillips Fox in Sydney in 1913. Hence the painterly vigour of Phillips Fox's *The ferry*, 1910-11, should be borne in mind when looking at such masterpieces as Gruner's *Morning light*, 1916, and *Spring frost*, 1919, (illus.) and even more so Wakelin's *The outcrop*, 1915, and *Down the hills to Berry's Bay*.

The 1910-20 period saw too the experimentation with abstraction in Australia, of which *Rhythmic composition in yellow green minor*, 1919, by Roy de Maistre (1894-1968) is an important example.

From this group of early modern Australian paintings there follows a sequence of large rooms, each more or less representing a period of between one and two decades. Between 1920 and the early 1940s it may be seen that Margaret Preston (1875-1963) made the most assertively modern images of the 1920s with *Implement blue*, 1927, (illus.) and *Western Australian gum blossom*, 1928; Eric Wilson (1911-47) fashioned the most ambitious cubist picture in Australia with *Abstract-the kitchen stove*, 1943; and *Study for dog gymkhana*, 1939, by Frank Hinder (born 1906), a tempera painting only occasionally displayed because of its fragility, and *Portrait of Grace Cowley*, 1939, by Ralph Balson (1890-1964) represent committed experiments towards abstraction in the late 1930s.

The modern era has often tended to be stamped too strongly with the notion of artists turning their backs on the past. The 1920s and 1930s saw many Australian artists of considerable ability and imagination who reflected on classical themes, visions of an untroubled arcadia, or the simple, intimate surroundings of everyday life. The sculpture *Fawn and nymph*, 1924, by George Rayner Hoff (1894-1934) and the paintings *Breakfast piece*, 1936, by Herbert Badham (1899-1961), *Into the light*, c.1938 by Percy Lindsay (1870-1952), and *Leda*, 1939, by Arthur Murch (born 1902) attest the variety of concerns of artists in the Australian collection of this period.

Moreover the poetic qualities of Tom Roberts' *Sherbrooke Forest*, 1924, Sydney Long's *The morning moon*, 1937, and Elioth Gruner's *Weetangera, Canberra*, 1937, are not diminished by comparison with the younger generation of painters. They show that the pastoral landscape tradition was well and truly alive in Australian art until the Second World War.

The main characteristic of the modern Australian collection up to this point is the predominance of art

BERTRAM MACKENNAL
Australian 1863-1931
Sarah Bernhardt (c.1893)
bronze relief
43.2 x 40.6cm
Bequest of Mrs J.A. McGregor
1944

E. PHILLIPS FOX
Australian 1865-1915
The ferry (c.1910-11)
oil on canvas
114.6 x 152.4cm
Purchased 1949

ELIOTH GRUNER
Australian 1882-1939
Spring frost 1919
oil on canvas
131 x 178.7cm
Gift of F. G. White 1939

opposite
ARTHUR BOYD
Australian born 1920
The expulsion (detail)
1947-48
oil on hardboard
99.5 x 119.6cm
Purchased 1986

MARGARET PRESTON
Australian 1875-1963
Implement blue 1927
oil on canvas on paperboard
42.5 x 43cm
Gift of the artist 1960

produced in Sydney. The next section begins with a small but important group of paintings by Melbourne artists. The modern movement in Melbourne is focused on the work of Arnold Shore (1897-1963), William Frater (1890-1974) and, although through his school perhaps rather than his painting, George Bell (1896-1966). Shore's *The park*, 1941, Frater's *Bush road near Anglesea*, late 1950s, and Bell's *Reclining nude*, 1937, represent the post-impressionist approach to painting that was being practised by that influential group from the 1930s in Melbourne.

In close proximity are other Melbourne paintings: *In the waiting room*, 1943, and *At the start of the march 1932*, 1944, by Noel Counihan (1913-86); and *Portrait of Mr I. Segal*, 1944, by Josl Bergner (born 1920). These are works of the social-realist school which flourished in Melbourne during the early 1940s. Nearby too is a splendid group of early paintings by Arthur Boyd (born 1920), including one of his most famous of the period, *The mockers*, 1945, and perhaps his greatest painting, *The expulsion*, 1947-48 (illus.) both typifying the artist's career-long interest in combining biblical or ancient mythological subject-matter with an Australian setting.

Beyond this group the Australian collection is once again dominated by Sydney artists, reflected in the large and rich holdings of paintings by Russell Drysdale (1912-81) and William Dobell (1899-1970), although

RUSSELL DRYSDALE
Australian 1912-1981
Sofala (1947)
oil on canvas on hardboard
71.7 x 93.1cm
Purchased 1952

it is important to bear in mind the connection between Drysdale and the George Bell School where he studied in the late 1930s. There are no finer holdings of the paintings of these two major Australian artists. Dobell's portrait *Dame Mary Gilmour*, 1957, (illus.) and Drysdale's landscape, *Sofala*, 1947, (illus.) are just two of their numerous masterpieces in the collection.

Other important works of the 1940s period include the surrealist painting *Archaeopteryx*, 1941, by Eric Thake (1904-82), the equally surrealist but less light-

hearted *The sower*, 1944, by James Gleeson (born 1915), *Boats at St Tropez*, 1944, by Weaver Hawkins (1893-1977), *Man with the yellow shirt*, 1944, by Justin O'Brien (born 1917), *Near the docks*, 1946, by Sali Herman (born 1898), *Still life*, c.1945-50, by Godfrey Miller (1893-1964), *Pretty Polly Mine*, 1948, (illus.) by Sidney Nolan (born 1917), the sculpture *Birth of Venus*, 1944, by Lyndon Dadswell (1908-86), and *Madame Sophie Sosostris (a Pre-Raphaelite satire)*, 1947-48, (illus.) sculptured by Robert Klippel (born 1920) and

WILLIAM DOBELL
Australian 1899-1970
Dame Mary Gilmore 1957
oil on hardboard
90.2 x 73.7cm
Gift of Dame Mary Gilmore
1960

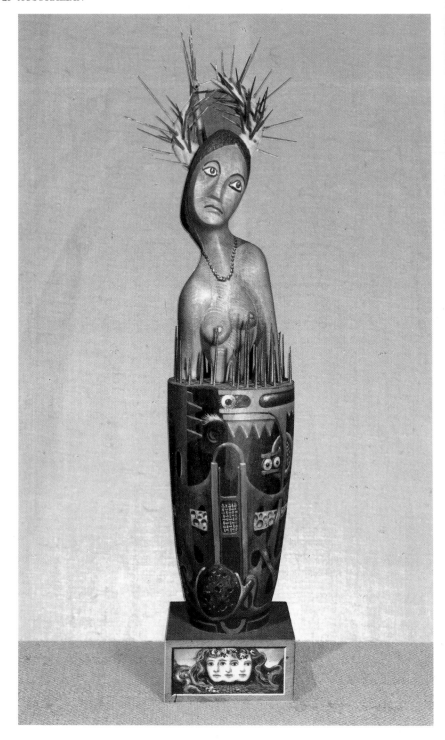

SIDNEY NOLAN
Australian born 1917
Pretty Polly Mine 1948
enamel on hardboard
91 x 122.2cm
Purchased 1949

SALI HERMAN
Australian born 1898
Sydney 1942-1981
oil on canvas
91.8 x 137.4cm
Gift of the artist 1981

painted by James Gleeson. This is only a small selection from an abundance of work of the 1940s in the Australian collection.

The Australian display is distinguished at various points by groupings of a number works by one artist: for example George Lambert, Margaret Preston, Grace Cossington Smith, William Dobell, Russell Drysdale and Sali Herman. The reason for this is that, rather than reflecting many decades of balanced scholarly insight, the Australian collection is really a history of often personal perception and opinion, of frank bias and occasionally political influence. Its character has been thus shaped, some artists acquired in depth, and others in a more token way. Accordingly, the display often cuts across the broadly chronological sequence with groups of works by one artist.

The paintings by William Dobell shown together range from his early 1930s works in London, with small jewel-like street scenes, interiors and head studies, to his portraits of the late 1950s; those by Sidney Nolan from his strange *Boy in township* of 1943 to *Burke,*

opposite
ROBERT KLIPPEL and
JAMES GLEESON
Australian born 1920
born 1915
Madame Sophie Sosostris (a
Pre-Raphaelite satire) 1947-48
painted wood
49.5 x 10 x 10cm
Gift of James Gleeson and
Robert Klippel 1970

LLOYD REES
Australian born 1895
Road to Berry 1947
oil on canvas on pulpboard
34.6 x 42.2cm
Purchased 1946

*c.*1962, where he brilliantly exploited the mythology of early Australian history; and Grace Cossington Smith's finest work, *Interior with wardrobe mirror,* 1955, (illus.) is displayed with her earlier paintings of the 1920s and 1930s. In each of these cases, it has been deemed more illuminating to keep the artist's works together rather than to distribute them among broad chronological displays.

Moving into the post-1950 period of the Australian collection a large number of works by the distinguished landscape painter Lloyd Rees (born 1895), who has lived some sixty years of his working life in Sydney, are displayed. They range from his *Road to Berry,* 1947, (illus.) to *Gerringong landscape,* 1952-56, and *Fire haze at Gerringong,* 1980, and are a testament to one of Australia's most sustained and inspired artists of the twentieth century. The Gallery's display of the works of Rees are the celebration of a great Australian artist in the city where he deserves to be seen in strength.

The key year for the 1950s period of the Australian collection is 1953. It was then that a major exhibition of contemporary French art came to Australia and, especially in Sydney, stirred painters once again towards abstraction. By 1956 abstract painting was in full force, with an ever stronger interest by artists in the subconscious impulse, and the autonomy of the work of art exclusive of the world of natural appearances. This may be seen in the works of both older and younger artists of the period: John Passmore (1904-84), whose paintings moved from the Cézannesque *Orange dot,* 1953, to the almost completely abstract *Jumping horse-mackerel,* 1959; John Olsen (born 1928) in his *Dry salvages,* 1956, responding to

LLOYD REES
Australian   born 1895
A tribute to France   1969
oil on canvas
116.9 x 132.1cm
Purchased 1969

**GRACE COSSINGTON
SMITH**
Australian   1892-1984

Interior with wardrobe
mirror   1955
oil on canvas on paperboard
91.4 x 73.7cm
Purchased 1967

Sydney Harbour, the poetry of Dylan Thomas and the writings of T. S. Eliot; the British-born itinerant Ian Fairweather (1891-1974) whose *Anak Bayan*, 1957, and *Roi soleil*, 1952-57, were inspired by his experiences in South-East Asia and are amongst his best paintings. There are also important works displayed from the 1950s Australian collection by artists with little Sydney connection. Ian Fairweather, mentioned above, lived for more or less the last twenty years of his life on an island off the coast of Queensland, although it should be remembered that his work was exhibited regularly in Sydney and its presence had a profound effect on the younger artists living here. Albert Tucker (born 1914), John Brack (born 1920) and John Perceval (born 1923), on the other hand, are almost exclusively associated with Melbourne; Tucker's *Apocalyptic horse*, 1956, Brack's *Nude with two chairs*, 1957, and Perceval's *Briar and dry creek*, 1960, are each quite key paintings in the respective developments of those artists.

Jon Molvig (1923-70) was a Brisbane-based artist, and he too is well represented in the collections. The darker side of his expressionist vision, blended with a fascination for the indigenous mythologies of Aboriginal culture, is perfectly realised in *Ballad of a dead stockman*, 1959.

The energy of the abstract movement of the 1950s gathered momentum in the following decade: John Olsen's *Spanish encounter*, 1960, and *New reality*, 1961, by Peter Upward (1923-83) contain between them an energy of gesture that is echoed later by Tony Tuckson (1921-73) in his *White lines (vertical) on ultramarine*, (1970-73), and Stanislaus Rapotec (born 1913) in his *Magnificat III*, 1983. John Olsen's later painting, *Nightfall when wattle stains the doubting heart*, 1979, combines with *The balcony (2)*, 1975, (illus.) by Brett Whiteley (born 1939), to affirm that the more gentle distillation of poetry of place into paint also has been an intrinsic part of art in Sydney since Tom Roberts and Arthur Streeton were here in the 1890s.

The influence of place and poetry is also an essential ingredient of the later work of Colin Lanceley (born 1938), and it is interesting to find the roots of it traced back from his *Where three dreams cross between blue rocks (Blue Mountains)*, 1983, to *Glad family picnic*, 1961-62. The earlier painting is an untidy but vivaciously inventive concoction, representing a period when Lanceley and his friends Mike Brown (born 1938) and Ross Crothall (born 1934) railed against the current tenets of painting by encompassing collage, found objects and popular images into their work.

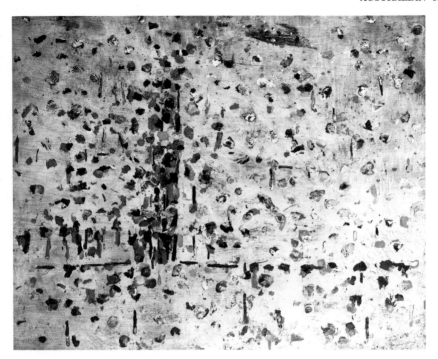

These works of the 1950s and 60s illustrate a certain coalescing of energies and interests between artists of the time, but include certain individuals who were really not part of the Australian scene for long periods. Francis Lymburner (1916-72) and Louis James (born 1920) both lived, as John Passmore had previously, for many years in England. Lymburner's painting *The studio corner, c.*1964, and James' *East of the moon (2),* 1962, are both quite brilliant summations of the gifts of those two artists.

Yet again the art of Sydney predominates in the last section of the Australian collection, although the works of Michael Johnson (born 1938), John Firth-Smith (born 1936), Ann Thomson (born 1933), Judy Cassab (born 1920) and Kevin Connor (born 1932), are juxtaposed with those of Melbourne artists Jan Senbergs (born 1939), Michael Shannon (born 1927) and Peter Booth (born 1940). Included here too are the majestic late paintings of Roger Kemp (1908-87) in *Archetype,* 1981, Jeffrey Smart (born 1921) in *Truck and trailer approaching a city,* 1973, James Gleeson in *The arrival of implacable gifts,* 1985, Fred Williams (1927-82) in *Waterfall polyptych,* 1975 and John Brack (born 1920) in his *Portrait of Fred Williams,* 1979-80, which is interesting to compare with the haunting

FRED WILLIAMS
Australian 1927-1982
You Yangs landscape 1963
oil on hardboard
119.5 x 152cm
Purchased 1980

BRETT WHITELEY
Australian born 1939
The balcony 2 1975
oil on canvas
203.5 x 364.5cm
Purchased 1981

Portrait of John Perceval, 1985, by Clifton Pugh (born 1924).

Fred Williams, who along with Roger Kemp was an elder statesman of painting in Melbourne during the last decade of his life completed a circle with the landscape tradition of the Heidelberg school, and is represented in the Gallery by works of exceptional quality, from *Sherbrooke Forest,* 1961, and *You Yangs landscape,* 1963, (illus.) to *Waterfall polyptych.*

All this of course deals with the most readily visible aspect of the Australian collections. There remains the wealth of the Gallery's holdings which are in storage and which can only be shown occasionally, perhaps because of space limitations, or difficulties of installation, or the fragility of their material. Most important of these are the Australian watercolours.

Ever since the Gallery officially established its

collections by commissioning a watercolour from
Conrad Martens in 1874, it has continued to acquire
Australian works of art in this medium to the present
day. The strengths of the Australian watercolour
collection are especially notable from the early
twentieth century up to the Second World War with
masterpieces by Norman Lindsay (1878-1969),
J. J. Hilder (1881-1916), William Blamire Young (1862-
1935) and Hans Heysen (1877-1968), and in recent
decades by Donald Friend (born 1915), Peter Purves
Smith (1912-49), John Olsen and Lloyd Rees, to name
just a few. But whenever artists have excelled in
watercolour, in all periods of Australian art, the Gallery
has usually secured at least one fine representative work.
Australian watercolours are shown in rotation for a
few weeks each year within appropriate areas of the
display.

European

Greek, Cycladic
c.2,500-2,000 BC
Female figure
marble
height 62.2cm
Gift of the Art Gallery Society
of New South Wales 1971

FRANCESCO DI SIMONE
FERRUCCI
Italian 1437-1493
Madonna and Child c.1480
marble relief
71.2 x 55.9 x 11.5cm
Purchased 1971

From its establishment in the 1870s the policy of the Art Gallery of New South Wales in so far as European art is concerned has been to acquire contemporary works. A most fortunate consequence of this activity in the nineteenth century and the early decades of the present century, was the development of a rich and quite outstanding collection of late Victorian painting, Edwardian painting and, subsequently, of modern British art. Whilst the overall scope of the European collection is medieval to modern, with occasional exceptions such as the *Cycladic figure* of c.2500BC (illus.), the British collection of the late nineteenth and early twentieth centuries remains a distinctive strength.

In the more recent past the emphasis in acquisitions has shifted towards enhancing the non-British European collection with a modest representation of a limited number of important paintings from Impressionism onwards.

The Old Master collection is housed in yellow ochre coloured rooms in the old wing of the building. Of the Renaissance works the marble relief *Madonna and Child* by Francesco di Simone Ferrucci (1437-93) (illus.)and *Madonna, Child and saints* by Sano di Pietro (1406-81) are noteworthy and exemplify the distinctive styles of Florence and Siena in the later fifteenth century. The group of sixteenth and seventeenth-century pictures is notable for the Dutch and Italian works that reflect the influence of Caravaggio. Of these the most outstanding is the recently cleaned Bernardo Strozzi (1581-1644) *The release of St. Peter*, painted in Venice in the mid-1630s (illus.). The watercolour gallery, which leads off from the Old Master collection maintains changing displays from the Gallery's representative collection of European watercolours

BERNARDO STROZZI
Italian 1581-1644
The release of St Peter
c.1635-40
oil on canvas
124.5 x 113cm
Purchased 1966

WILLIAM HOGARTH
English 1697-1764
Dr Benjamin Hoadly, MD
early 1740s
oil on canvas
75.8 x 63.8cm
Purchased 1951

which includes a J. M. W. Turner (1775-1851) *High force: fall of the Trees, Yorkshire*, 1816-18 (illus.), and occasionally from the collection of Australian watercolours.

The eighteenth-century gallery displays portraits on one side, of which William Hogarth's (1697-1764) *Dr. Benjamin Hoadly MD*, early 1740s, (illus.), Joshua Reynold's (1723-92) large and imposing *James, 7th Earl of Lauderdale*, 1759-61, and Robert Edge Pine's (1730-88) similarly large *The young sportsman*, 1766, are particularly worthy of note. On the opposite wall are displayed eighteenth- and ninteenth-century works which, with the attendant sculptures, evoke a Golden Age in the styles of Neo-Classicism and Renaissance revival. Richard Wilson's (1714-82) *St. Peter's and the Vatican from the Janiculum, Rome*, 1757, recalls Nicholas Poussin in its romantic and arcadian view of the Campagna, whilst John Glover's (1767-1849) landscape, n.d., recalls Claude in much the same vein. Continuing the theme is John Constable's (1776-1837) *Landscape with goatherd and goats*, 1823, which is one of two copies that the artist made of Claude's *Landscape with goatherd and goats* painted in c.1636, and William Etty's (1787-1849) *The golden age*, c.1840, which shares that same Neo-Classicism but with a more distinctive Victorian aesthetic.

The yellow ochre corner gallery with classical marble sculptures is a meeting point for three areas, the Old Master section, the Victorian gallery and the tribal art gallery which is approached down the marble staircase. The mood of Classicism continues from the late eighteenth-century paintings into the Victorian era. The mid-Victorian sculptures by American and English artists come from the collection of Judge Josephson, Sydney, 1892, who ordered them from the artists living in Italy. John Gibson's (1790-1866) works form an important group, together with the work of two of his pupils, the American Harriet Hosmer, and Benjamin Spence. Gibson's early *Narcissus* shows the soft sensuous flesh of Canova, whilst his later *Hunter and dog*, (1860s), (illus.) is in a more severe, idealized Greek style. Hosmer's (1830-1908) sculpture depicts *Beatrice Cenci* (1577-99) who was beheaded for plotting her wicked father's death and was imprisoned with her stepmother at 'La Petrella', a lonely castle on the road to Naples. Gibson's *Hunter and dog* looks towards the Victorian court, and across to the opposite corner gallery which contains bronzes of the later Victorian period from the 1870s. Smaller paintings are also displayed in these two corner galleries.

The Gallery's fine collection of Victorian and Edwardian paintings are displayed in the large galleries painted a Pompeian red, the original wall colour. The first of these large courts, which leads on from the Old Master galleries, is hung with Edwardian

J. M. W. TURNER
English 1775-1851
High force: fall of the Tees, Yorkshire 1816-18
watercolour
28.3 x 40.3cm
Purchased 1949

paintings on one wall (sometimes Victorian) and large pictures from the Royal Academy exhibitions in London and Paris Salons on the other. Of the former group Frank Cadogan Cowper's (1877-1958) *Faust's first sight of Marguerite*, 1915, is an enchanting picture inspired by the famous conclusion to Act 1 of the opera *Faust* and, in Cowper's interpretation, also by the Bride's Door at St Sebald's in Nuremburg. Unusual too is the fact that this picture was commissioned by the Board of Trustees of the Gallery in 1912. The seductive world of privileged society in Edwardian England is perfectly captured in many of the works displayed in this section of the Gallery and particularly in Phillip Wilson Steer's (1860-1942) luxurious portraits of *Mrs. Violet Hammersley*, 1906-07, and of Miss Montgomery in a painting entitled *The beaver hat*, 1907. Edward Poynter's (1836-1919) portrait of *The Hon. Violet Monckton*, 1899, is a more classic but nonetheless evocative expression of that Edwardian ideal. The Gallery has a particularly strong representation of the work of Steer and, among the landscapes, *Ludlow Castle*, 1898, is particularly noteworthy for its energetic brushwork in the artist's so-called 'choppy' style.

The Royal Academy and Salon paintings on the opposite wall are classic examples of the heroic and dramatic style of the genre. Luminais' *The Sons of Clovis*, 1880, is a distinguished if daunting picture illustrating the punishment of the two sons of the King of France in having their tendons cut for rebelling against their father. The often overwhelming and heroic style of late nineteenth-century British and French Academy painting is similarly illustrated in the sentiment of Briton Riviere's (1840-1920) *Requiescat*, 1888, Alphonse de Neuville's (1835-85) clamorous *The defence of Rorke's Drift* and François Sallé's *The anatomy class;* all large and dominant works which are seldom removed from the permanent displays.

In the second corner gallery and throughout the large Victorian courts are dispersed a number of late Victorian and Edwardian bronzes and marbles representative of the new English school of sculpture. Of these, works by Alfred Gilbert (1854-1934) and Gilbert Bayes (1872-1953) predominate; with a further representation of French sculptures including Jean Antoine Injalbert (1845-1933), Antoine Bourdelle (1861-1921) and Agathan Leonard (1841-?). The latter's work is evocatively echoed in paintings of the New English School, particularly E. H. Maxence's beautiful rendering of two medieval sisters in *Le Livre de Paix (The Book of Peace)*.

opposite
JOHN GIBSON
English 1790-1866
Hunter and dog
Fourth replica 1860s
marble
119.7 x 88.8 x 54.4cm
Bequest of Judge Josephson
1892

FREDERIC LEIGHTON
English 1830-96
Cymon and Iphigenia 1884
oil on canvas
163 x 328cm
Purchased 1976

The Gallery's outstanding collection of works representing the Victorian Olympians is displayed in these same courts. The greatest exponent of the style, Lord Leighton (1830-96), is well represented by, among others, three paintings of particular distinction: *Cymon and Iphigenia*, *Wedded*, 1882, and *Winding the skein*, c.1878. In the latter painting Leighton expresses a neoclassic emphasis in the draughtsmanship that combines with a romantic sensuousness of colour, bathed in a clear Mediterranean light, to create a dreamlike sense of nostalgia. Indeed the Elgin marbles furnished models for one of the figures in *Winding the skein*. *Cymon and Iphigenia*, c.1884, (illus.) is not a classical myth, but a story of Boccaccio. Cymon is depicted at the moment of transformation from a rough shepherd to a lover of beauty and knowledge by the unexpected sight of Iphigenia asleep. The dawn of

love, and the illumination in his soul is paralleled
by the moon beginning to rise and shed its bluish
light on a scene still warm from the summer sun.

The masterpiece of Leighton's most distinguished
follower, Edward Poynter (1836-1919) is *The visit of
the Queen of Sheba to King Solomon,* 1884-1890,
(illus.) which was purchased in London in 1892 and
since its acquisition has virtually never been off display.
This massive and imposing picture is full of exquisite
detail, the result of Poynter's superb draughtsmanship
and the meticulous studies he undertook for every
figure in the finished work. His archeological
reconstruction is based on long study of the wonders
then being brought to the British Museum, but calls
upon his own imagination to create the Temple of
Solomon, thereby showing his intention to make the
work an architectural and decorative unity with its

original frame.

A more recent acquisition is George Frederic Watt's (1817-1904) *Artemis and Hyperion*. This profound and mellow picture describes Hyperion, God of the Sun, seated on a cloud with Artemis, Goddess of the Moon. It is, in the manner of the Victorian Olympians, a painting with a classical theme and a sense of grandeur, but also a pervasive air of mystery.

The Pre-Raphaelite collection, displayed in the adjoining court, is dominated by Ford Madox Brown's (1821-93) magnificent *Chaucer at the Court of Edward III*, 1845-51, (illus.), which remains the most famous work in the European collections. Brown lamented, when he thought the picture had been destroyed in the fire that engulfed the International Exhibition Building in Sydney in 1852, that it '... took up the better part of five years of my early manhood'. Of interest too is that in his diary Brown mentions a number of sitters for the painting, including Dante Gabriel Rossetti as Chaucer and Emma, the artist's second wife, as Johanna the fair maid of Perth and as Philippa, the wife of Chaucer. In the same area are displayed other Pre-Raphaelite works, notably Spencer Stanhope's (1829-1908) *Why seek ye the living among the dead*, 1870s or *c*.1890, Edward Burne-Jones' (1833-98) *St. George kills the dragon* (1864 or 66) and John Strudwick's (1849-1937) *A story book*, 1883-84.

The aesthetic movement is the basis for further displays in the area which include such moving paintings as John Everett Millais' (1829-96) *The Captive*, 1882, William Margetson's (1861-1940) delicate and romantic portrayal of an auburn-haired, classically robed woman entitled *The sea hath its pearls* and James Tissot's (1836-1902) *The widower*, 1876, (illus.) of which Oscar Wilde wrote '... it is full of depth and suggestiveness; the grasses and wild, luxuriant growth of the foreground are a revel of natural growth...'

The pensive mood of Aestheticism is seen in a very different light in the realist and naturalistic styles of the late Victorian era, displayed in the adjoining room. Luke Fildes' (1843-1927) *Widower*, 1876, (illus.) and Stanhope Forbes' (1857-1947) *Their ever-shifting home*, 1887, are emotive expressions of concern on social conditions and poverty that provide a stark contrast to the grandeur of the Pre-Raphaelite subjects. William McTaggart's (1835-1910) Scottish impressionist work *Rainy day, Carradale Harbour*, 1883, presents a rather different view of life; a life of harmony and natural beauty as the fishermen prepare their boat.

The influence of French *plein-air* painting, and of

opposite
JAMES TISSOT
French 1836-1902
The widower 1876
oil on canvas on hardboard
118.1 x 76.8cm
Gift of Mr & Mrs Colin
Anderson 1939

S. LUKE FILDES
English 1843-1927
The widower 1875-76
oil on canvas
168.9 x 248.3cm
Purchased 1883

the realist painter Bastien-Lepage in particular, is seen in the good representation of works by George Clausen (1852-1944) and Henry La Thangue (1859-1929) of which *Cider apples, c.*1899, is the most notable. The French sources may be seen in Gaston La Touche's (1854-1913) *The first born*, 1888, whilst the popular 'orientalist' theme is well illustrated in the wonderfully exotic *Snake-charmer*, 1889, by Alphonse Etienne Dinet (1861-1921), a painting that was acquired in the early years of the Gallery's history, in 1890.

The European galleries in the new wing house the collection of impressionist and post-impressionist paintings in the Gallery collections. Claude Monet's (1840-1926) *Port Goulphar, Belle-Ile* and Camille Pissarro's (1830-1903) *Peasants' houses, Eragny*, (illus.) both painted in 1887, are the most distinguished. A major purchase, Pierre Bonnard's (1867-1947) *Self-portrait, c.*1940, (illus.) began something of a new era in the Gallery's collecting attitude. The acquisition of this painting coincided with the opening of the Captain Cook wing in 1972 and highlighted the need to strengthen the representation of early twentieth-century European art. The Bonnard self-portrait was painted when the artist was seventy-three and affirms his vision of light and colour as the subject of his painting style. His own personality seems veiled in the shadow behind reflecting light. Other early twentieth-century paintings on view include works by Andre Derain (1880-1954), Albert Marquet (1875-1947), Henri Hayden (1883-1970), Jean Lurcat (1892-1966),

GEORGES BRAQUE
French 1882-1963

Houses and trees 1909
oil on canvas
64.5 x 54cm

Purchased 1980

CAMILLE PISSARRO
French 1830-1903

Peasants' house, Eragny 1887
oil on canvas
59 x 72.1cm

Purchased 1935

Fernand Leger (1881-1955).

Towards the end of the 1970s and in the 1980s the Gallery acquired several important works which illustrate the significance of developments in European art in the years before the outbreak of World War I. George Braque's (1882-1963) *Houses and trees*, painted in 1909 (illus.), is a critical moment in the evolution of analytical Cubism; Vasily Kandinsky's (1886-1944) watercolour *Study for Painting with white border* was painted in 1913 when his imagery finally loses its character of depiction, and form and colour free

PIERRE BONNARD
French 1867-1947
Self-portrait *c.*1940
oil on canvas
76.2 x 61 cm
Purchased 1971

MAX BECKMANN
German 1884-1950
Old woman in ermine 1946
oil on canvas
150.5 x 80.5cm
Second AGNSW Foundation
Purchase 1987

themselves to suggest abstract and spiritual effects; and Ernst Ludwig Kirchner's (1880-1938) *Three bathers*, 1913, (illus.) shows Kirchner at his most mature and the German expressionist movement at its most pervasive moment in a society on the brink of war. The German representation was strengthened with the purchase in 1987 of Max Beckmann's (1884-1950) *Old woman in ermine*, 1946, (illus.) a symbolic, characteristically deeply expressive work painted in Amsterdam in 1946.

In 1981 the Gallery acquired its first Pablo Picasso (1881-1973). *Nude in a rocking chair* (illus.) was painted in Cannes, on 25 March 1956 when Picasso was seventy-five. The nude can be recognized as Jacqueline Roque who was to become his second wife. She is seated in a bentwood rocker in the studio of his new villa 'La Californie' at Cannes, the palm tree in the garden visible through the French doors. It shows Picasso as

ERNST LUDWIG
KIRCHNER
German 1880-1938
Three bathers 1913
oil on canvas
197.5 x 147.5cm
First AGNSW Foundation
Purchase 1984

opposite
PABLO PICASSO
Spanish 1881-1973
Nude in a rocking chair 1956
oil on canvas
195 x 130cm
Purchased 1981

SPENCER GORE
English 1878-1914
The Icknield Way 1912
oil on canvas
63.8 x 76.8cm
Purchased 1962

an expressionist violently painting the struggle between man and woman, artist and model.

The modern British collection presents a relatively comprehensive view of British painting of the twentieth century, highlighted by some quite outstanding pictures such as Spencer Gore's (1878-1914) *Icknield Way*, 1912, (illus.), *Sunflower and sun*, 1942, by Paul Nash (1889-1946) *The suffragettes*, 1943-4, by Victor Pasmore (born 1908), a number of works by Samuel Peploe (1871-1935), *The interval before round 10*, 1920, by William Roberts (1895-1980), *Christ in Cookham* by Stanley Spencer (1891-1959) and *Welsh Mountains* by Graham Sutherland (1903-80). Walter Richard Sickert (1860-1942) spans the nineteenth- and twentieth-centuries with his early works such as *Gatti's Hungerford Palace of varieties*, c.1887-8, and the later works hanging in the new wing. Of particular note are representations of British schools or groups. The Camden Town School is well illustrated by Spencer Gore; English Cubism by William Roberts and Percy Wyndham Lewis (1882-1957); Scottish Cubism by the works of Samuel Peploe and J. D. Fergusson, whilst the rich and expressive colours of Matthew Smith's (1879-1959) *La chemise jaune*, c.1925, and a number of Augustus John (1878-1961) paintings, including a 1918 portrait of the Australian Prime Minister, William Morris Hughes, give real depth to the sombre richness of early twentieth-century British art.

In the decades between the end of World War I and the 1950s the multiplicity of styles and directions taken in British art is illustrated in the 'primitive' works of Christopher Wood and Winifred Nicholson; the blend of Neo-Romanticism and Neo-Surrealism is

HENRY MOORE
English 1898-1986
Helmet head No 2 1950-53
bronze
height 34.3cm
Purchased 1955-6

PERCY WYNDHAM LEWIS
English 1882-1957
Figure composition 1912
pen and ink, watercolour,
gouache
30.5 x 21cm
Purchased 1983

shown by Sutherland, Spencer and Nash; the decorative style in the work of Tristram Hillier (1905-83); Abstractionism in Ben Nicholson's (1894-1982) *Still life*, 1946, and the genteel figurative expressionism of British art of the 1940s in the work of Ivon Hitchens (1893-1979) and William Scott (born 1913).

Of the more recent British art, of the 1950s and onwards, the most outstanding works are Francis Bacon's (born 1910) *Study for self-portrait*, 1976, one of a group of works representing a violent expressionist distortion of the figure, Alan Davie's (born 1920) *Flag dream no.4: wheel*, 1957, Patrick Heron's (born 1920) *Big rumbold orange*, undated, and Frank Auerbach's (born 1931) *Primrose Hill, autumn*, 1984. The most recent works are sometimes displayed in the galleries of contemporary art. Mention should also be made of important European sculptures in the collection which include Henry Moore's (1898-1986) *Reclining figure: angles*, outside the Gallery, Marino Marini's (1901-80) *Horse and rider*, and Philip King's (born 1934) *Blue between*, 1971.

Aboriginal

Aboriginal art today is now recognized as being diverse, expanding and changing, and, in many ways refusing to be defined. The Art Gallery of New South Wales has probably one of the best-integrated collections of Aboriginal art in Australia. The collection began in a pioneer venture by the then Deputy Director of the Gallery, Tony Tuckson, who believed that Aboriginal art belonged in the Art Gallery and should be considered as art rather than as items of ethnography.

In 1956 the Gallery received a gift from the Commonwealth Government of paintings on cardboard collected by Charles Mountford during the 1948 American/Australian scientific expedition to Arnhem Land. The bulk of the collection of over 200 bark paintings was acquired for the most part between 1959

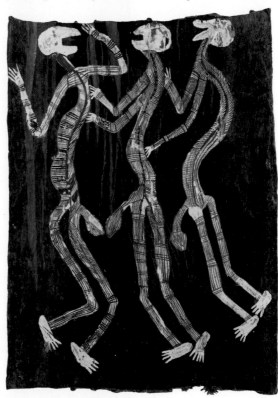

WAGBARA
Croker Island
Three Mimi spirits dancing
bark painting
76.2 x 54.6cm
Purchased 1964

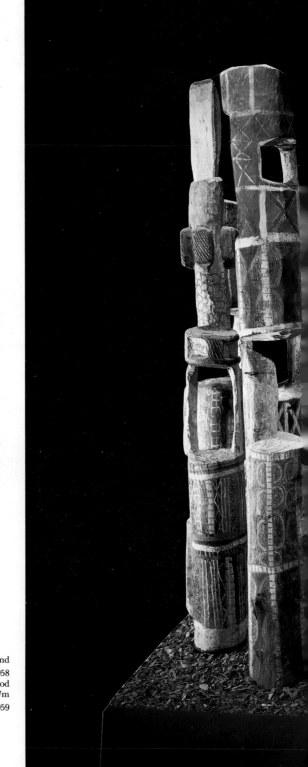

Snake Bay, Melville Island
Seventeen grave posts   1958
carved and painted wood
maximum height 2.7m
Gift of Dr S. Scougall 1959

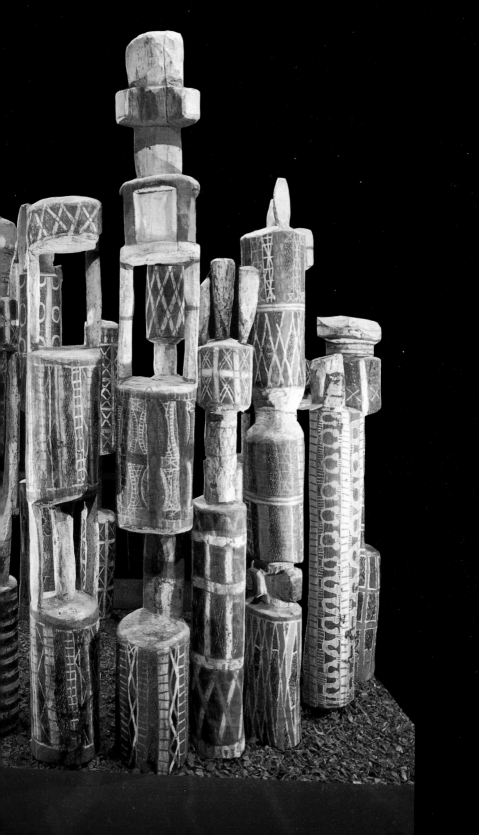

ARTIST UNKNOWN
Groote Eylandt
Dugong hunt
bark painting
45.7 x 96.5cm
Gift of the Commonwealth
Government 1956

and 1962 by Tony Tuckson, with the practical and financial support of Dr Stuart Scougall. Visiting northern Australia, including the Tiwi Islands and Arnhem Land in 1959, they commissioned the set of seventeen grave posts and many bark paintings.

Aboriginal art is in the main religiously inspired. The array of bark paintings, sculpture and other items are linked by major religious creation stories. Though the x-ray figure type of bark painting from Western Arnhem Land (illus.) is thought of by many as 'the' bark painting style many different styles exist depending on the area of origin. Individual artists also stamp their own personal style in each painting. From the east, Yirrkala, are several series of monumental barks depicting the major creation stories of the Dhuwa (illus.) and Yirritja (illus.) moieties. Further east again are the refined fragile figures of the velvet black manganese, paintings of Groote Eylandt (illus.). From the western area of Port Keats where bark painting is a relatively new art form is a small group of spotted landscapes (illus.).

Aboriginal art is both personal, temporary, and event-orientated, many designs painted on bark being body designs or sand sculptures for ceremonies. Many fragile totemic sculptures, which are either worn or employed in ritual dances, are made of bark bound with string and fixed with feathers and resin or wax representing animal or human spirits. Each painting whether on bark, sculpture, or utilitarian item is more than a painting: it represents a ceremony, a song or dance, a place, a time, a person.

The centre piece of the sculpture collection is the group of massive and profound Pukamuni Poles cut from iron wood (illus.) and commissioned from the Tiwi people of Bathurst and Melville Islands. These

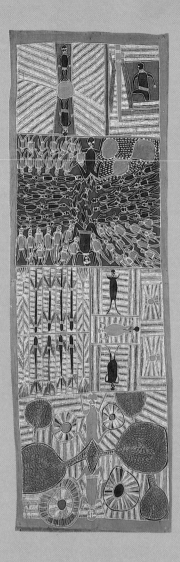

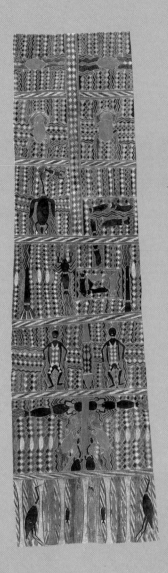

MAWALAN
1908-67
Riradjingu Miliwuwur,
Dhuwa moiety
assisted by others

Djang'kawu myth
bark painting
188 x 64.8cm

Gift of Dr S. Scougall 1959

YANGGARIN
born 1932

Dalwongu group, Yirritja
moiety

Barama and Lainjun
bark painting
275.6 x 80cm

Gift of Dr S. Scougall 1964

MILINGIMBI
Arnhem Land
Totemic sculptures
painted paperbark, string,
wood and feathers
maximum height 64.7cm

Purchased 1962

grave posts are painted and cut with traditional designs
and represent the ancestors and relatives of the dead.
Bark baskets painted in the same fashion and placed
on the poles are part of the same Pukamuni ceremony:
the funeral rite.

Another group of similar but hollow poles are from
Arnhem Land where a death and funeral ceremony,
the Hollow Log/Bone Coffin ceremony, is held. In
this ritual the bones of deceased people are cleaned,
sung over and placed in a specially decorated Hollow
Log (illus.). The Log is painted with clan designs much
the same as the body of living and dead Aborigines
are painted at times of special revelation. It is placed
upright in the public camp and then left.

A series of human and human-like spirit figure
sculptures exist in the collection. Carved from types
of soft wood the figures, like the short Yirrkala
sculptures and the Malangi carving (illus.), represent
original creative beings and are derived from, if not
directly similar to, pieces used in ceremonies. More
recent additions have been the spectacular, thin Mimi
figures from western Arnhem Land by Gurdal. These
are also used in certain ceremonies. Several small
figures from Melville Island are decorated representing
real people prepared for a Pukamuni ceremony.

The bulk of the collection was acquired prior to
the 1970s before the advent of Western Desert painting
on canvas. Two spectacular examples of the inspiring
new genre of Aboriginal art, one by Clifford Possum

MARDIGAN
Port Keats
Billabongs
bark painting
63.2 x 37.8cm
Gift of Dr S. Scougall 1961

Tjapaltjarri and Tim Leura Tjapaltjarri, (illus.), the other by Jack Phillipus Tjakamarra, have recently been acquired by the Gallery. The movement started when Aboriginal artists from Papunya were taught to transfer their traditional 'sand painting' designs on to canvas with acrylic paints. This has now spread across the Western Desert, and other centres such as Yuendumu, Kintore and Lajamanu are also thriving and the whole movement has added new depth to an ancient culture.

With the inevitable movement of Aboriginal peoples to the urban centres of Australia yet another source of inspiration has been added to Aboriginal art. In the last decade or so many urban Aboriginals have been moved to seek inspiration in their traditional arts, but have expressed that inspiration in a style and manner that reflects their now de-tribalized way of life. Jeffrey Samuel's *A changing continent* is an example of this new direction in Aboriginal art.

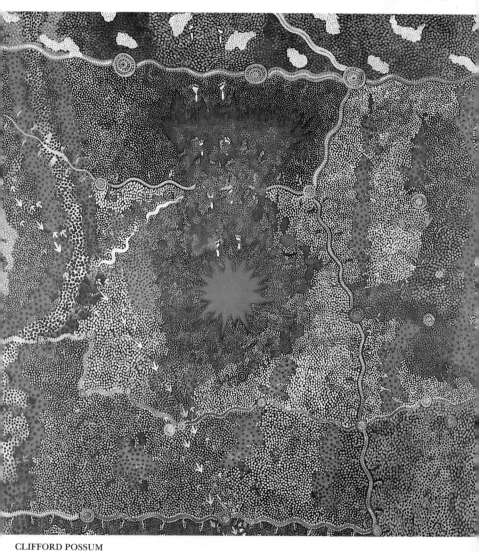

CLIFFORD POSSUM TJAPALTJARRI
assisted by his brother, TIM
LEURA TJAPALTJARRI
Anmatjera tribe

Warlugulong
acrylic on canvas
168.5 x 170.5cm

Purchased 1981

Melanesian

The Melanesian collection was formed in the 1960s and early 1970s, and shows the variety of art styles from the different racial and language groups of the area.

Examples include art from the Solomon Islands, Irian Jaya and Papua New Guinea. Of special interest are the Solomon Islands canoe prow (illus.) and the pre-historic stone figure (illus.).

New Guinea

Of particular importance is the gift of the late S. G. Moriarty of his New Guinea Highlands collection. This was the largest and most important private collection from this region. Stan Moriarty described the art he collected in these extracts from his notes and publications:

> The great diversity of tribes, languages and customs shows greatly in decorative head-dresses and general material culture . . .
>
> There is little wood carving. Masks, until recently, were made mostly of gourds, the rest in bark, tapa cloth, tree fern, palm fronds and mud modelled over a fibre frame. The gourds are usually round to oval, one side being cut away so that the larger section would fit over the wearer's face. They are mostly painted and often decorated with feathers, Job's tears, human teeth, cuscus fur, moss from the rain forest and a host of other materials . . .
>
> Few figures are carved in the round and are usually in traditional dress and with ornaments attached. Some are placed on the side of the road as images of deceased ancestors, some are located in the gardens to watch over the corpse and also act as decoys. Others are placed as decoys in the passageway of the men's house at North Fore, Okapa, Eastern Highlands. As they are around 1.5m high, in a night attack they would look realistic and a spent arrow would give the alarm to the occupants of the house . . . [illus.]
>
> In parts of the Western and Southern Highlands human hair wigs were worn as part of the everyday dress, each area having its particular wig style. In some cases they were a status symbol. Hats are also worn usually for ceremonial occasions. There seems to be no limit to the number of styles of feathered head-dress for which the Western Highlands are noted . . . Nature provides a wealth of materials for the dress and ornamentation of the body.

New Guinea, Long Island,
Bok Village
Female figure
basalt
29.9 x 12.1cm
Gift of the Art Gallery
Society of New South Wales
1969

opposite
Solomon Islands

Canoe prow ornament
wood, stained black,
inlaid pearl shell
ht. 31.7cm
Purchased 1962

New Guinea Highlands
Figures from the S. G. Moriarty
Collection
carved wood
average height 150cm
Purchased with funds donated
by S. G. Moriarty 1977

Asian

The Gallery's collection of Asian art encompasses many aspects of the diverse culture of the Far East (China, Korea and Japan), India and South-East Asia. The genesis of the collection was a large gift of Japanese ceramics and bronzes presented by the Japanese Government after the 1879 International Exhibition held in Sydney. Subsequent to that the Asian holdings grew through gift, bequest, and some purchases, until the establishment of a distinct Department of Asian Art in 1979. The purpose of this introduction is to represent the entire collection by highlighting what are regarded as the best of the different traditions and periods that come under the umbrella definition of 'Asian'.

The first culture encountered on entering the Asian gallery is that of China, represented by a chronological presentation of works of art dating from the Shang dynasty (c.1600-1027BC) and earlier, through to the twentieth century. A strength of the display of early Chinese art, which is to be found to the right of the entrance, is the collection of earthenware funerary pieces (*mingqi*). A legacy of the Chinese practice of elaborate tomb burials, *mingqi* silently convey to us detailed information concerning the style of ancient Chinese culture and civilization. Fine examples of *mingqi* in the Gallery's collection include the single standing figure of a lady of the Han dynasty (206BC-220AD), the elegant and elaborately gowned pair of court ladies of the Tang dynasty (618-906AD) (illus.) and the model of horse and rider decorated in the three colours of cream, green and amber familiar to Tang glazed tomb figures and referred to as *sancai*, literally three colours. The manner of the display is intended to echo the way in which such figures were grouped in niches in the approaches to the subterranean burial chambers.

Many pieces on display bear testimony to the pervasive influence of Confucianism, Daoism and Buddhism, the three ideologies responsible for the aesthetic, iconographical and symbolic attitudes reflected in Chinese visual arts. The first two are indigneous to China. Buddhism reached China from India about the first century BC, attaining its greatest strength and wealth in the eighth century, and

bestowing on the world a wealth of Chinese images and symbols inspired by its canons. Free-standing sculptural examples of Buddhist deities in the Chinese collection are the limestone figure of a Bodhisattva (a potential Buddha) of the Tang dynasty and the wooden figure of Guanyin (the Goddess of Mercy) of the Song dynasty (960-1279AD).

Dating to the Ming dynasty (1368-1644) is the commanding and belligerent Buddhist figure of the military Bodhisattva Wei To, his flowing robes barely concealing his armour underneath, his arms flexed and ready to use the weapon he once held. Such guardian figures as this were placed at the entrances to Buddhist

Chinese, Tang
dynasty c.700 AD
Figure of court lady
earthenware with painted
pigments
ht. 36.5cm

Gift of Sydney Cooper 1962

monasteries and Wei To's powerful stance, costume and fierce expression all affirm his appropriateness as a guardian figure.

The symbols associated with these ideologies so fundamental to Chinese civilization naturally became absorbed into the repertoire of decorative features for her art. Buddhist and Daoist symbols, for example, abound in the ornament to be found on Chinese ceramics, the tradition which forms the strongest representation of the decorative arts of China. The chronologically arranged displays illustrate the history of the ceramic tradition from the painted pots of the Neolithic era, to the perfection of form characteristic of Song ceramics, the subtle hues of celadons, the colourful inventiveness of the Ming dynasty and the richness and diversity of the Qing dynasty (1644-1911).

One of the highlights of the ceramic displays is the collection of Ming porcelains. It is in porcelain that the Chinese potters excelled, particularly from the fifteenth century when imperial patronage was the catalyst for the establishment of special kilns at Jingdezhen in southern Jiangxi province. The Emperor Xuande (reigned 1426-35) himself reportedly took a keen personal interest in the fifty-eight kilns at Jingdezhen occupied with filling the imperial orders and the blue and white porcelain of this period is considered the finest ever made. The Xuande period is represented by a stemcup made for imperial use (illus.). Such cups were almost solely used for Buddhist rituals and intended to be placed on an altar before the image of a Buddha or Bodhisattva and filled with clear water. The decoration on the bowl of this stemcup is appropriately Buddhist: the eight Buddhist emblems each surmounting a lotus bloom, the Buddhist symbol of purity. An extremely rare piece of Chinese blue and white porcelain is the Hongzhi period (1488-1505) plate with the uncommon design of dragon in waterweeds.

Chinese ceramics were produced for both the local and foreign markets, with shapes and designs being modified accordingly. On display are Ming pieces produced for the South-East Asian, Japanese and European markets. For example, the Swatow ware dish with a freely drawn phoenix design typifies the vitality and spontaneity of export pieces whose comparative roughness is the preferred choice of some to the unrivalled perfection of imperial pieces. Examples of the blue and white porcelain produced for the Japanese market (termed *kosometsuke*) are also on display. While marked by a similar casual, albeit sparser, sense of design, such pieces are distinguished by the imperfections of an 'insect eaten' (*mushikui*) edge, an effect admired by Japanese connoisseurs.

The European market was insatiable in its demands for Chinese porcelain with huge quantities being exported from the Ming throughout the succeeding Qing dynasty (1644-1911). Some pieces were decorated in Chinese taste, others were produced solely to European orders, and still others, such as the Gallery's Monteith bowl, with its Chinese style decoration and European silver shape, were a beguiling mix.

The largest section of the Gallery's Chinese ceramic collection is that representing the Qing dynasty. The veneration for the past, a characteristic reflected throughout the history of Chinese art, reached its height in the Qing dynasty. Imitations of antique wares were produced throughout the dynasty and archaistic designs became increasingly popular. For example, the fine elliptical bottle of the Qianlong period (1736-95) (illus.), is modelled on the classic fifteenth-century 'moon flask' prototype. Archaistic designs are exemplified in the Qing ceremonial vessels of canonically determined shapes and colours such as the yellow altar vessels the *zun* and *dou* for which the designs and decorations are based on bronzes of the Western Zhou dynasty (*c*.1100-71BC).

New technical developments in the Qing dynasty augmented the palette available to potters. This is exemplified in the group of *famille verte* pieces on display, in which the predominant colour is green. Fine pieces in the Gallery's collection include the large vase brilliantly decorated with ladies in a garden

Chinese Ming dynasty
Xuande period (1426-35)
Stemcup
porcelain decorated in
underglaze blue
ht. 10cm
diam. of mouth 11.9cm
Purchased 1979

setting, and the pair of vases with integral stands. Interesting is the Daoist decoration that appears on the *famille verte* dish depicting Xi Wangmu, Queen Mother of the West and guardian of the peaches of immortality (illus.).

As early as the fifth century, Chinese critics had identified *qi* (spirit) as the first essential of painting. Particularly after the rise of the literati painting (*wenrenhua*) in the latter half of the eleventh century, the emphasis of painting tended to be on self-expression, on the subjective and individualistic, beyond any restrictions imposed by aiming for verisimilitude or technical meticulousness. Quintessentially, Chinese painting is the language of the individual through the brush, the mark on paper. This emphasis on the expressionistic use of ink on paper is to be seen in all the Chinese paintings in the Gallery's collection, a selection of which are always on display in the Chinese section. Modern Chinese painting, which is the focus of the Gallery's collection, began in Shanghai in the nineteenth century. An important contribution of the Shanghai school was to extend the subject matter from the traditional emphasis on landscape to encompass figures, portraits, birds and animals, flowers and plants.

Chinese Qing dynasty
late Kangxi period
early 18th century
Large dish
porcelain decorated in
famille verte enamels
diam. 39.6cm
Gift of Mr J. H. Myrtle on the
occasion of the opening of the
new Asian gallery 1988

Wu Changshuo (1844-1927), an early Shanghai master, concentrated on flowers or boughs with blossom or fruit (illus.). His painting is bold and energetic, and he enjoyed the rich expressive value of layers of ink on paper. That same mature energy is to be seen in Wu's expressive but controlled calligraphy. Another modern painter who studied nature meticulously was Qi Baishi (1863-1957) (illus.). His paintings brim with life, vitality and freshness while in his use of colours he skilfully draws upon the vivid colours of Chinese folk art.

The Japanese collection comprises many paintings

Chinese, Qing dynasty
Qianlong period (1736-95)
from Jingdezhen, Jiangxi province
Moon vase
porcelain decorated in underglaze blue and red
ht. 30.5cm
Purchased 1964

WU CHANGSHUO
Chinese   1844-1927

Loquats   1919
hanging scroll; ink and colours
on paper
181.5 x 82cm

Purchased 1987

opposite
QI BAISHI
Chinese   1863-1957

Gourds on trellis
hanging scroll; ink and colours
on paper
137 x 61cm

Purchased 1986

which will form part of a changing display in the Japanese section of the Asian gallery. Japanese culture converges and diverges from the mainland culture of China. Like China, it was the recipient of Buddhism, as shown in our displays by the twelfth-century image of Amida, the Buddha who reigns over the Western Paradise (illus.). Regarded as the personfication of eternal life, compassion and boundless light, Amida was one of the most fervently worshipped deities in Japan. Like most Japanese sculpture, this example is made of wood which the native Japanese sensitivity for materials has always seemed to prefer. The sculpture

Japanese 12th century

Figure of Amida Buddha
nutmeg wood
ht. 53cm (with base 96.5cm)

Purchased with assistance from
the W. H. Nolan Bequest Fund
1984

has a presence beyond its physical size, and its sense of volume and aura of serenity are characteristic of sculpture of the glorious aristocratic age of the later Heian period (894-1185) when it was constructed.

Zen Buddhism was another sect of Buddhism that came to Japan from China, bringing with it a new style of ink monochrome painting (*suibokuga*) characterized by the skilful manipulation of brush and ink. The *suibokuga* tradition is well represented in the Gallery's collection by paintings such as the pair of screens by Unkoku Tōeki (1591-1644) (illus.). In accordance with the native Japanese sensitivity to the nuances of nature, the screens allude to seasonal and temporal changes, with the right screen depicting spring/summer in the morning and the left screen depicting autumn/winter in the evening. While many aspects of these screens, for example, the Chinese style pavilions and figures, and the virtuoso control of ink tones, follow the prescribed axioms of the *suibokuga* tradition, the irrepressible touches of the artist's own personality add a piquancy to our enjoyment of the screens. In the same *suibokuga* style are another pair of landscape screens by the influential and important genre artist Kusumi Morikage (*c*.1620-90).

Zen too was the inspiration behind the painting by Kyoto artist Nagasawa Rosetsu (1754-99) of the two famous Zen eccentrics, Kanzan and Jittoku (illus.). Tradition has it Kanzan was a hermit-poet in Tang dynasty China who befriended the nearby temple's kitchen help Jittoku who gave him left-over temple food, a kindness Kanzan repaid by reading his poems to Jittoku. Rosetsu has brilliantly captured the

UNKOKU TŌEKI
Japanese 1591-1644
Landscape
pair of six-fold screens; ink, slight colour
and gold wash on paper
each screen 154.5 x 353cm :
Purchased with funds donated
by Kenneth Myer 1986

psychological interaction between the two friends. Every bit as eccentric, amusing and energetic in its brushwork is Soga Shōhaku's (1703-81) portrait of the poet Rinnasei. This scroll illustrates Shōhaku's ebullient, often wayward, but always deeply moving calligraphy.

The Edo period (1615-1867) in Japan saw the development of a townsmen's culture and the concomitant growth of indigenous styles of painting characterised by bright colours and a preference for the decorative and narrative. This tendency is perfectly illustrated in the pair of screens known as *Rakuchū rakugai zu,* the generic name for a specific type of Japanese painting which originated in Kyoto during the sixteenth century and reached its apogee in the seventeenth century. Such screens are significant not only for accurately portraying the various architectural and scenic spots of Kyoto, but also for their lively, often amusing, depiction of the everyday activities and customs of Kyoto citizens.

The most famous of the various schools of painting catering to the tastes of the townfolk would be that of *ukiyo-e.* Literally meaning 'pictures of the floating world', *ukiyo-e* derived originally from a Buddhist term referring to the transitory pleasures of life on this earth. Subjects of *ukiyo-e* tend to focus on the courtesans and entertainers of the pleasure quarters of cities and Kabuki actors. The Gallery holds a few fine examples of *ukiyo-e* painting: the small, finely painted screen, euphemistically entitled *Merrymaking in the garden,* in which the viewer voyeuristically enjoys the interior of a pleasure house (illus.), and the emotive portrayal of a courtesan by Katsukawa Shun'ei (1762-1819) In this rare painting Shun'ei (better known as a printmaker) has sensitively captured the introspection of his subject, who, about to be free of the entertainment district, is contemplating the ten years of hardship she has spent there. Other *ukiyo-e* works in the collection include works by Watanabe Nangaku (1767-1813), Kubo Shumman (1757-1820) and a particularly outstanding scroll by Miyagawa Chōshun (1683-1753) depicting a male actor in a female role for the Kabuki theatre (illus.).

The more decorative of the purely Japanese traditions, the Rimpa School, is represented in similarly distinguished works of consummate and delicate beauty by Suzuki Kiitsu (1796-1858) and Sakai Hōitsu (1761-1828). The Kyoto-oriented Maruyama-Shijō School is represented again by a number of works including an eye-catching pair of screens depicting white cranes against a gold background by Maruyama

opposite
NAGASAWA ROSETSU
Japanese 1754-99
Kanzan and Jittoku *c.*1787
hanging scroll; ink on paper
157.7 x 81.8cm
Purchased 1985

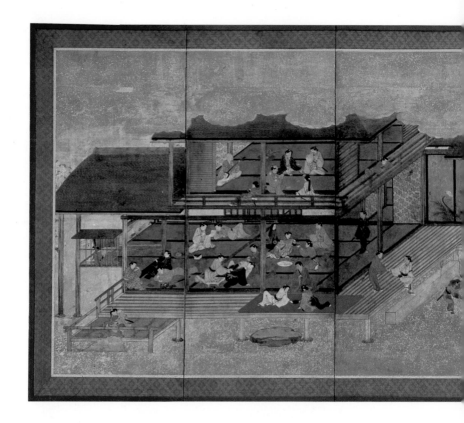

Ōkyo (1733-1775), from whom the school took its name.

On a more intellectual and sublime level than *ukiyo-e* is the magnificent landscape by Tani Bunchō (1763-1840) (illus.). Formerly in the collection of a feudal lord (*daimyo*), this painting, reiterating the persistence of Chinese-inspired painting traditions, presents the viewer with a serenely grand and atmospheric scene articulated through a virtuoso use of brush and ink. That same Chinese-inspired landscape is well illustrated in the collection in scrolls by leading artists such as Matsumura Goshun (1752-1811), Ikeno Taiga (1723-1776), Sō Aiseki (?-1837), Fugai Honkō (1779-1847), Takahashi Sōhei (1802-35), Ki Baitei (1734-1810), Tsubaki Chinzan (1801-54) and a pair of screens by Yamamoto Baiitsu (1783-1856).

While the display of screens and scrolls in the Japanese section will be constantly changing, ceramics

will constitute a permanent display. Arranged mainly chronologically, the earliest piece in the collection dates to the Yayoi period (*c.*200BC-250AD). Yayoi pottery is characterized by an emphasis on form with only minimal decoration, and large, impressive jars such as the Gallery's example were made for special events such as harvest festivals.

From the medieval period to the present, the aesthetics of the tea ceremony have shaped the Japanese appreciation of ceramics. Through the style of tea ceremony termed *wabi* or 'poverty' tea and its espousal of qualities such as *sabi* (literally 'rust' or 'patina'), and *shibui* (quiet, unobstrusive elegance), the Japanese have evolved an aesthetic canon based on the appreciation of the understated, monochromatic, asymmetrical and ephemeral. These qualities are to be seen in many of the ceramics on display, as well

Japanese   mid 17th century
Merrymaking in the garden
six-fold screen; colour on gold leaf paper
62.2 x 209.2cm
Purchased 1986

TANI BUNCHŌ
Japanese 1763-1840
Early summer mountains in
the rain 1826
hanging scroll; ink on paper
174 x 96cm
Purchased with funds donated
by Kenneth Myer 1987

opposite
MIYAGAWA CHŌSHUN
Japanese 1683-1753
Standing figure of an actor
hanging scroll; colours on
paper
110 x 53cm
Purchased by the Art Gallery of
New South Wales Foundation
1987

as in the Zen-inspired ink paintings. Important tea ceremony wares represented in the collection include examples from the Shigaraki, Shino and Bizen kilns. A balance to 'tea taste' is seen in Japanese porcelains of which two pieces in the Gallery's collection are especially noteworthy. These are the Ko-Kutani bottle (illus.), and the Kakiemon dish both of which relish colours and images sparsely arranged on a white ground.

Largely through the generosity of the Rev. Mune-

haru Kurozumi, the Gallery has a good and growing collection of contemporary Japanese ceramics comprising over forty pieces by a variety of noted contemporary potters (illus.). The display of a selection of these pieces concludes the Japanese section of the display.

Linking the Chinese and Japanese displays is an area devoted to Korea. The peninsular nation of Korea absorbed much from China and also acted as a conduit for transmitting mainland culture to Japan. Because of its turbulent history, much of its material culture has been destroyed, but a unique contribution to world culture is the celadon ware of the Koryo period (918-1392) which is so justly admired for its glaze, colour and elegance. The Gallery has several Korean celadons, of which the finest is a shallow dish with an incised design of parrots.

The Indian and South-East Asian collections are displayed in a separate section of the Asian gallery. In India, Hinduism as well as Buddhism was an inspiration for artists. The Indian collection contains some fine sculptures, for example the intricately carved relief of the Hoysala period (twelfth-fourteenth centuries), originally a wall panel on a Hindu temple (illus.). The relief depicts the Hindu god Śiva on the left, accompanied by the seven mother goddesses (Mā trkās). The mother goddesses represent inimical spirits:

KANESHIGE TŌYŌ
Japanese 1896-1967
Bizen ware
Tea bowl
height 7.8cm   diam. of mouth
12-12.6cm
Gift of the Rev. Muneharu
Kurozumi 1986

Japanese   late 17th century
Ko-Kutani ware
Bottle
porcelain
ht. 20.1cm
Purchased 1979

they are dangerous, malevolent beings whose behaviour, particularly to children under sixteen, is consistently violent. Worship of them is aimed primarily at deterring them.

The Hindu influence, so obvious in the cultures of India and some South-East Asian societies, is also to be seen in the Javanese image of Ganeśa, the popular elephant-headed Hindu god of good fortune and prosperity (illus.). Here his corpulent body is seated on a double lotus throne with the soles of his human feet touching. The snake and the elaborate head dress with a crescent moon and skull indicate his close association with the Hindu god Śiva. Originally his four arms would have held his attributes: a broken tusk, a fly whisk, a rosary and a cup of sweets.

An imposing sculpture in the South-East collection is the Khmer guardian lion dating to c.1000AD (illus.). Free standing lions such as this were conspicious features of the magnificent Hindu temple complexes built by the Angkor kings when the Khmer empire was at its peak from the tenth to twelfth centuries. Such lions were placed on terraces and stairways to guard the central pyramidal structure that symbolized Mt Meru, the residence of the gods at the centre of the Hindu world. This single monumental piece evokes the mysterious timeless majesty of a temple compound. Its characteristic full frontal pose with firmly planted front legs give the figure a composed regal air, while in the elaborately carved demonic head and patterned chest can be seen the Javanese influence so important to the development of Khmer culture.

Khmer ceramics exude a similar presence of serenity and majesty that belies their smaller size. Made solely for the local populace and not for export, they unfortunately had completely disappeared by the fourteenth century due to the fierce competition offered

Thai 13th-14th century
Sankampaeng ware
Jar
stoneware
ht. 28cm
Gift of Mr F. Storch 1986

by the technically superior, imported Chinese celadons and porcelains. However extant pieces offer a unique facet of the Asian ceramic tradition as exemplified by the elephant shaped jar (illus.), which demonstrates the popularity of zoomorphic vessels in the Khmer repertoire, as well as the significance of the elephant in the world of ancient Cambodia, where it was used for work as well as for ceremony.

The Gallery's expanding collection of Thai art contains several examples of ceramics, as well as smaller bronze Buddha images. Noteworthy among the ceramics is the attractive Northern Thai jar that has been identified as a product of the Sankampaeng kilns (illus.).

Later Thai taste is reflected in Bencharong ('five colour') ware, a porcelain that was made and decorated in China in accordance with Thai taste. The rich variety of enamel colours found on these ware was the result of technical developments in China in the eighteenth century, particularly the creation of the *famille rose* family which employed pinks made from a precipitate of gold.

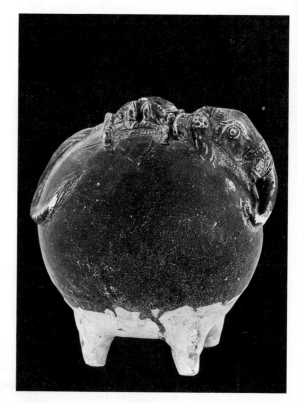

Khmer 11th-12th century
Elephant-shaped jar
stoneware
ht. 21cm
Purchased 1981

Khmer *c.*1000 AD

from Koh Ker
Guardian lion
sandstone
ht. 84cm

Purchased 1987 with funds
donated by
Ross H. Adair
T. R. W. Allen
Carl Berkeley
Bruce R. Bockman
Madeleine Boulken
Joanna Capon
Graham M. Cole
S. M. Gazal
Bruce C. Hudson
Rodney T. Hudspeth
Daryl Isles
J. G. Jagelman
N. Jeffreson
Michael Magnus
D. A. M. McCathie
Rosalind O'Connor
Lesley Pockley
G. & E. Sternberg
F. Storch
Robert Whyte
Ken Youdale

Contemporary

The Art Gallery of New South Wales' Department of Contemporary Art was founded in 1979. Purchases were of course made prior to that time, but it has been in the period since then that a lively exhibition programme and acquisition policy have been promoted and consolidated. The exhibitions have included the biennial show of contemporary Australian art, 'Australian Perspecta', various group shows and 'mid-career' surveys and the Gallery's participation in the Biennale of Sydney which focuses on recent international art. The Department has been able to pursue a more developed acquisition programme for Australian art with the generous bequests in memory and honour of Henry Salkauskas and Rudy Komon; the Evatt Foundation Purchase and the Mervyn Horton Bequest, which is specifically for overseas art. This latter donation has already brought the work of such celebrated artists as Anselm Kiefer, Mimmo Paladino, Guilio Paolini, Cindy Sherman, Philip Guston, and others to the Gallery.

At this stage the collection focuses upon work which has evolved since the 1960s. It is clear, however, that the strength of the collection lies in the more recent practices of the 1980s. The greater emphasis on overseas contemporary art in the collection has permitted comparisons and contrasts with the expanding body of contemporary Australian art. Such juxtapositions reflect the increasing role that Australian art is playing in the international spectrum. It will be clear as one moves through the contemporary galleries, that purchases are in general made of established international artists, distinguished as well as younger Australian artists who are still in the early stages of their careers. The four galleries of the contemporary wing will be rearranged every three months in order to explore new juxtapositions. Hence, it is only possible here to discuss some highlights of the collection rather than provide a permanent guide to each room. This reflects the changing nature of contemporary art and the shifts which occur in its critical assessment.

Of course, there have been a considerable number of artistic trends initiated in the period since the 1960s: Minimalism, Conceptualism, Pop Art, Arte Povera, Fluxus, Environmental Art, Neo-Expressionism, the Transavantgarde, to name some of the more significant

FRANK AUERBACH
British born 1931
Primrose hill, Autumn 1984
oil on canvas
121.9 x 121.9cm
Mervyn Horton Bequest Fund
1985

ones. They are tendencies which have sought to challenge, undermine, reassess or replace orthodox notions of art. The Department of Contemporary Art was established when most of these had run their course and so there are no outstanding representations of these trends, with the notable exception of Mimmo Paladino (born 1948), an Italian Transavantgarde artist whose *Cordoba,* 1984, (illus.) demonstrates the recent tendency for transgressing various avant-garde movements and amalgamating cultural symbols. Most of the above movements have, however, deeply influenced some of the significant purchases which are discussed below.

Perhaps the most significant example of American abstraction in the collection is Morris Louis' (1912-62) *Ayin,* 1958. Louis is considered a post-painterly abstractionist whose reductive use of the medium and emphasis on objecthood contributed to the seeds of Minimalism. Louis created veils of thin, diluted, gentle washes of acrylic colour, staining the unprimed canvas

FRANK STELLA
American born 1936
Khurasan gate 1970
acrylic on canvas
304.8 x 914.4cm
Gift of the Art Gallery Society
of New South Wales 1977

and allowing the colour to sink in. While the surface is completely flat, the glow and sheer depth of the painting are apparent. The reductive, non-gestural impulse is perhaps even more obvious in *Khurasan gate,* 1979, (illus.) by Frank Stella (born 1936) where his geometrical abstraction is determined by the shape and structure of the canvas. It is an important example of Stella's protracta series. Both these works are a fitting beginning for the contemporary collection and an appropriate link between it and Australian art because both Louis and Stella reacted against the painterly and gestural abstraction of the 1940s and 1950s and prefaced Minimalism which has had a sustained effect on art until the present day.

The Gallery also has a substantial collection of contemporary British art. Added to the biomorphic colour abstraction of Patrick Heron (born 1920) are recent works by an older generation of British artists whose painting has recently reasserted itself. Frank Auerbach (born 1931) and Leon Kossoff (born 1926) have developed a sophisticated gestural expressionism. Auerbach's *Primrose Hill (autumn),* 1984, (illus.) typifies his dense, spontaneous brushwork which often describes the intimate world of friends, family and familiar locations, integrating the surface texture and the subject through a luscious scaffold of strokes. Even though Auerbach may rework the paint, scraping it

MIMMO PALADINO
Italian born 1948
Cordoba 1984
oil on canvas
300 x 400cm
Mervyn Horton Bequest Fund
1987

back each day if he is not pleased, he miraculously maintains the fresh appearance. The work lives and breathes as the gestures simultaneously fix the landscape in place and splinter off into a surface frenzy of rich crimsons, dark reds and golds as if to predict further versions of the landscape.

Kossoff also paints friends, but he embeds them in a thickly encrusted surface, the wrinkled paint almost sagging on the canvas. At times there is an inherent contradiction in his work between the permanency, presence and patina of age in the paint and the ephemeral nature of the image.

Anselm Kiefer is one of the leading figures in contemporary European art. Born in Germany in 1945, he became a student of the influential Joseph Beuys. Kiefer has been identified as a neo-expressionist but he actually stands outside trends. His works are very unusual, especially his technique of building up the paint over photographic paper and working on it with a blow torch to create a textured, abrasive surface. Although Kiefer makes paintings, he is as much a sculptor in the tradition of Arte Povera and Fluxus. Kiefer's use of materials is highly symbolic and alchemical, despite their literal presence. *Glaube, hoffnung, liebe*, 1984-86, (illus.) has a charred surface, perhaps an impression of the Baltic seashore with the waves bashing the rockface in the upper part of the image. Kiefer's rendition of the space is not as simple, however: the lead propellor attached to the canvas

LEON KOSSOFF
British born 1926
From 'Cephalus and Aurora'
by Poussin No 3 1981
oil on hardboard
92.7 x 129.5cm
Purchased 1984

ANSELM KIEFER
German   born 1945

Glaube, hoffnung, liebe
1984-86
emulsion, synthetic polymer
paint, shellac
on photo-document paper on
canvas with lead
280 x 380cm

Mervyn Horton Bequest Fund
1986

simultaneously lies upon the surface, as if it has crashed, and also hovers above it, so that the viewer's reading of the perspective is confused.

The three blades of the propellor are inscribed in chalk with the three Christian virtues: Faith, Hope, Charity. There is a contradiction between the optimism of Faith, Hope and Charity and the dismal, pessimistic

scene of a battered and scorched Europe. Kiefer's use
of chalk on lead is also a reference to Beuys whose
works often involve chalk on blackboards and who
was himself a World War II pilot.

Kiefer's painting is burdened with the brooding
layers of European history. Some critics have said this
artist revives dangerous elements of Romanticism and

GUILIO PAOLINI
Italian born 1940
L'altra figura 1984
plaster
183 x 250 x 190cm
Mervyn Horton Bequest Fund
1987

glorifies a nationalism and heroicism common to
Hitler's Germany. On the contrary, Kiefer carefully
confronts the past tragedy and seeks to retain what
is important for the soul, such as the legitimate cultural
history and mythology. His use of Jewish traditions
within an essentially Germanic landscape scarred by
time, the plough and the grenade, is calculated to bring
these issues into sharp relief.

Giulio Paolini (born 1940) is an Italian artist whose
conceptual and Arte Povera work has been well known
since the 1970s. *L'altra figura*, 1984, (illus.) is a
conceptual conundrum combined with formal
elegance. Two identical casts of a classical head mirror
each other, gazing sightlessly over their shoulders.
Between them on the floor lies the shattered remnants
of a third head. This arrangement could be compared
to the Narcissus myth in which the hero's reflected
image dissolved into broken fragments. The mirroring
and perpetual reproduction in this sculpture raises the
meaning of and quest for an original identity.

The British artist, Christopher Lebrun (born 1951),
like Paolini, turns to a mythical past. His *Untitled
(wreath II)*, 1984, (illus.) refers to the wreath worn by
victors and used as a motif in the classical friezes of
Pompeii. Lebrun's reaction against the abstract art that

dominated art schools where he studied, survives in the abstract gestures of the red area. On close inspection they transform into the image of a horse and chariot charging towards us. This image emerges like a vision or apparition and then dissolves again. By drawing on heroic imagery from European history, Lebrun is perhaps seeking to capture a unified visual culture which he feels has since been fractured.

O o otoph (the death of Ekim Rrap) in the wings of the oedipal theatre, 1985, (illus.) by the Australian artist Mike Parr (born 1945) is one of a number of major works by the artist in the collection. Parr has a history of conceptual and ephemeral art. This sculptural work is truly of the 1980s in that the conceptual notions play a major role in the installation. Installed in a room which can be viewed through a doorway is a wall which appears to be falling into the space, exposing the 4″ x 2″ beams. One section is already on the floor. The interior is lit by a single stark globe which trails the floor from a long white flex. The plastered wall has been rubbed back and the dust has settled on the floor. On the end wall is a characteristically squashed self-portrait. There is an

CHRISTOPHER LEBRUN
British born 1951
Untitled (wreath II) 1984
oil on canvas
254 x 289.5cm
Mervyn Horton Bequest Fund
1986

ROBERT OWEN
Australian born 1937
Appositiion 1979-1980
mixed media installation
273 x 613cm
Purchased 1983

MIKE PARR
Australian born 1945
O o otoph (the death of
Ekim Rrap) in the wings
of the oedipal
theatre 1985
mixed media room
installation
Gift of the artist 1985

KEN UNSWORTH
Australian born 1931
Free fall 1975
mild steel
225 x 200 x 200cm
Purchased 1979

extraordinary stillness and tension set up by these minimal elements. For most viewers the obvious impact is the psychological oppression of the space inside the room which echoes the compression of the portrait.

Robert Owen's (born 1937) *Apposition*, 1979, (illus.) is an installation consisting of photographs of a four-legged stool which has been captured in strong sunlight at various times of the day. Hence, the photographs trace the rotation of the shadow around the stool. These photographic canvases are accompanied by real stools casting dramatic shadows in the room. Owen has made the laws of the cosmos intimate by presenting them as shadows falling on an ordinary stool.

Pataphysical man, 1984, (illus.) is one of five works in the collection by the Australian artist Imants Tillers, who was born in Latvia in 1950. Tillers has an enduring interest in the reproduced image and our cultural dependence on it instead of originals. He also ridicules the accuracy of reproductions, often mimicking the out-of-register effect. In this painting he pillages Giorgio de Chirico's *The archeologist*, 1926-27, interspersing it with pieces from his own childhood, Latvian folk images and stories. His references to Aboriginal culture are apparent in the multiple white

handprints. In this, the artist identifies with the displacement of minor cultures in general. Perhaps the most characteristic element in Tillers' work are the canvas boards which are adhered to the wall to form the whole and can be stored in stacks. Tillers has exhibited these stacks as objects in themselves.

Lesen in staub, das wilde lieben, 1984, (illus.) by the Swiss artist Miriam Cahn (born 1949) is an extraordinary drawing evoking the powerful expression of prehistoric cave painting. Cahn, who now lives in Berlin, grates the charcoal onto the paper and draws in the dust with her fingers. The images she makes

are of children, animals and women. They are created, as it were, in the dark, by the sensation of touch. At the end she blows away the charcoal to reveal the image. Cahn's method asserts a female sensuality and lends a semi-conscious immediacy to the drawings.

Black bolero, 1980, (illus.) is by Miriam Schapiro (born 1923), an important American feminist artist who began working as an abstract expressionist. Schapiro changed her direction to combine the feminine intimacy of patchwork and embroidery with the heroic scale and shaped canvases of abstract painting. Schapiro has been a significant figure in the rediscovery

IMANTS TILLERS
Australian born 1950

Pataphysical man 1984
synthetic polymer paint, charcoal and pencil on 168 canvas boards
305 x 532cm

Ewan Murray Bequest Fund 1985

MIRIAM CAHN
Swiss born 1949
Lesen in staub, das wilde
lieben 1984
charcoal on paper
59.5 x 84cm each, 4 parts
Mervyn Horton Bequest Fund
1985

of decoration and pattern as a serious form of expression. This influence is visible in artists of all generations in New York, such as Frank Stella and Robert Kushner.

Cindy Sherman (born 1954) lives and works in New York City. She is represented in the collection by four untitled works from 1979 to 1982. Sherman, who photographs herself in various guises, acts as performer and photographer at once, and yet there are no narcissistic overtones in her work. Instead, her chameleon-like ability to change her character explores the social and cultural typecasting in contemporary society.

JOHN WALKER
British/Australian born 1939
Oceania — my dilemma 1983
oil on canvas
triptych, each panel 212 x
171cm
Purchased 1983

Susan Norrie (born 1953) is one of the more exciting artists working in Australia at the present time. Like Sherman, Schapiro and Cahn, she has an abiding interest in issues which affect women. *Fruitful corsage; bridal bouquet; lingering veils,* 1982-83, (illus.) is a

triptych exploring marriage. The shimmering rendition of pearls and diamonds, the opalescent white shells, flowers and fruit are combined in erotic juxtapositions. The forms metamorphose, curl, transform and shift under a veil of harsh light and an encrusted surface. The essence is one of extravagance and rich, fecund opulence, but haunting this triptych is a lingering sense of decay.

Like Norrie, the works of Melbourne painter, John Walker (born 1939) have an immense physicality. His monolith motif and foreboding insect dominate the gestural expanse of *Oceania — my dilemma*, 1983, (illus.). Walker animates the abstract icon so that it borders on figuration and imbues it with a spiritual resonance which is underlined by the biblical quotation. The title is a clear reference to the artist's interest in Oceanic art which has had a notable influence on the 'primitive' form of the stick insect.

Bill Henson (born 1955) is represented by a number of works in the collection all of which are *Untitled*. Perhaps the most striking of these is the group from 1983-84. Henson's photographic arrangements emphasize the series and continuum with his stress on triptychs and diptychs. In this particular series, Henson depicts a grandiose Baroque interior and *beaux-art* museums, the essence of aristocratic affluence, with scenes of victimized young women, abused, abandoned and smeared with blood and grime. Each image is treated in the same sensual, dense and evocative manner, the colour being reduced to near monochrome through successive screenings. His photographs are like glimpses into complex and tragic stories. His comparisons are often ironic as here where he critically equates contemporary social decay with Baroque decadence and links the concepts of desire and death

SUSAN NORRIE
Australian born 1953
Fruitful corsage; bridal bouquet; lingering veils   1983
oil on plywood
triptych, each panel 182 x 121cm
Henry Salkauskas Art (Purchase) Award Fund 1983

MIRIAM SCHAPIRO
American born 1923
Black bolero 1980
fabric, glitter, synthetic
polymer paint on canvas
182.9 x 365.8 cm
Purchased 1982

in images which are at once familiar, erotic and exotic.

The Australian artists Simone Mangos (born 1959) and Ken Unsworth (born 1931) both create sculptures and installations which possess an uneasy, evocative and at times eerie sensibility. Mangos's *Salt lick*, (1986), (illus.) alters with time as the rust from the nails invades the purity and complacency of the white salt while Unsworth's *Free fall*, 1975, (illus.) seems to defy gravity and preserve a precarious, threatening balance.

The Department of Contemporary Art is an expanding collection which will, appropriate to its very nature, shift and alter its focus with the corresponding advancements in recent art practice, providing deeper insights into current visual art.

SIMONE MANGOS
Australian born 1959
Salt lick 1986
salt, nails
34 x 34 x 30cm
Purchased 1987

Prints & Drawings

Drawings and prints are exhibited in the long gallery to the south in the new wing's level 2, under carefully controlled lighting conditions. On first entering, the lighting may seem very low after some of the more brightly lit painting galleries, but the eyes should soon adjust to this. Works of art made on paper are particularly fragile, and can be damaged by prolonged or undue exposure to light; so to ensure the preservation of the collections the Gallery has followed a policy of exhibiting any work on paper for no more than three months in any two-year period. Consequently the exhibitions will be changed every few months in a continuing cycle intended to display different aspects of this large and diverse collection.

FRANK HINDER
Australian born 1906
Dance of the Koshares, New Mexico 1933
drawing; pencil
33 x 43.8cm
Purchased 1967

The collection represents works of art in the European tradition from the High Renaissance of the late fifteenth and early sixteenth centuries to innovative work of recent years. There is a preponderance of Australian works, both drawings and prints, from the last hundred years and with a particular bias for most

GEORGE LAMBERT
Australian 1873-1930
Hugh Ramsay 1901
drawing, pencil
25.1 x 16.9cm
Purchased 1959

of that time towards Sydney artists. The smaller but developing European collections now allow a reasonably comprehensive view of the Western tradition, particularly as expressed in prints. Certain aspects of the Asian collection of works on paper, the earliest of which is a twelfth-century Japanese woodcut of images of the Buddha, are maintained with the prints and drawings collection.

At the Sydney International Exhibition of 1879 the English illustrated magazine *The Graphic* arranged a special pavilion; the first drawings bought for this Gallery in 1880 were chosen from that display. They were illustrator's drawings intended for reproduction through wood engraving, and provided examples of international quality for those Sydney artists who gained an income providing illustrations for local publications, notably for the *Bulletin*. Over the years, examples of Australian artists' drawings for the *Bulletin* — particularly by George W. Lambert (1873-1930) and Frank Mahony (1862-1917) — have been acquired and make an interesting comparison.

Before the end of the century, half-a-dozen French drawings and some drawings by Australian artists had been added to the collection and subsequently a large and fairly representative collection of twentieth-century Australian drawings has been formed. Its characteristic Sydney bias has led to particularly interesting groups of works by the gentle watercolourist J. J. Hilder (1881-1916) and the flamboyant George W. Lambert; the elegant Thea Proctor (1879-1966); the brothers Lindsay, Lionel (1874-1961) and Norman (1879-1969); the Sydney modernists Grace Crowley (1890-1970), Rah Fizelle (1891-1964) and Frank Hinder (born 1906); Eric Wilson (1911-46) and William Dobell (1899-1970), who studied in London in the 1930s; the influential Godfrey Miller (1893-1964) and John Passmore (1904-84); and the prophetic visions of Sydney and the landscape by Lloyd Rees (born 1895). Of particular beauty and invention is the group of nearly a hundred drawings and collages selected from an immense *oeuvre* created over a period of forty years by the sculptor Robert Klippel (born 1920).

This short survey.can only hint at the range of Australian drawings by many artists, both famous and little known. In addition to the artists linked with Sydney, there are monotypes and drawings by Rupert Bunny (1864-1947), drawings by Hans Heysen (1877-1968), Russell Drysdale (1912-81), Sidney Nolan (born 1917) and Eric Thake (1904-82). The collection is particularly indebted to continuing gifts and bequests,

ROBERT KLIPPEL
Australian born 1920
Drawing, December 1951
drawing; pen and ink, pencil and watercolour
37.5 x 54cm
Gift of the artist in memory of Marie Gardiner 1970

ERIC WILSON
Australian 1911-46
The artist and William Dobell,
London c.1938
pencil
20 x 15.5cm
Purchased 1958

THEA PROCTOR
Australian 1879-1966
The picnic 1925
drawing; pencil, watercolour
wash and body colour
40.6 x 56.5cm
Gift of Emmie Russell 1985

JEAN-HONORE
FRAGONARD
French 1732-1806
Orlando Furioso: Atlante,
mounted on the Hippogryph,
swoops down upon
Bradamante (late 1780s)
drawing; brush and brown ink
wash over black chalk
39.6 x 25.3cm
Purchased 1982

and especially to the gifts by prominent artists of their
own works. The nineteenth century, particularly before
the founding of the Gallery in 1876, is by contrast
not extensively represented although there are now a
few very fine drawings by John Glover (1767-1849).
S. T. Gill (1818-80), William Strutt (1825-1915), G. F.
Folingsby (1830-91) and Louis Buvelot (1814-88); most
of these are comparatively recent purchases.

There are only a few examples of European master
drawings: the most notable are two drawings by Jean
Honoré Fragonard (1732-1806) from a famous series
of some 137 sheets illustrating Ariosto's epic poem
Orlando Furioso (illus.) (a third drawing from this
series is in the National Gallery of Victoria, Melbourne). The fecund coupling of great poetry and
visual art has a long history and distinguished
offspring: Botticelli and Dante, Delacroix and
Shakespeare, Fuseli and Milton. The Fragonard
drawings for Ariosto are in this great tradition and

are the first works in the collection to represent the high flowering of eighteenth-century French culture.

There is a rather large representation of British drawings of the nineteenth and twentieth centuries, from the landscapes of John Sell Cotman (1782-1842), Thomas Monro (1759-1833) and Edward Lear (1812-88); studies by Lord Leighton (1830-96) and Edward Poynter (1836-1919) for their paintings in this collection; early twentieth-century works by Henri Gaudier-Brzeska (1891-1915) and Horace Brodzky (1885-1969), as well as the more established British school represented by William Orpen (1878-1931) and Augustus John (1878-1961).

An extraordinary series of drawings by Lyonel Feininger (1871-1956) was acquired in 1979. They date from almost every period of his working life, from his earliest cartoon drawings until shortly before his death. Acclaimed as the 'first cubist painter in Germany', he was one of the founding masters of the Bauhaus at Weimar in 1918, moving with it to Dessau in 1925 and finally returning to the land of his birth, the USA, in the mid-1930s. The Gallery also has a. significant group of work by another Bauhaus artist, Ludwig Hirschfeld Mack (1893-1965), who settled in Australia after World War II.

A small group of German and Austrian prints has been developed in recent years, with the eventual aim of showing other major early twentieth-century movements — the Secession, Expressionism, Dada. Beginning with Max Klinger (1857-1920) in the 1880s, the collection can now show examples by Edvard Munch (1863-1944), Egon Schiele (1890-1918), Oskar

EDVARD MUNCH
Norwegian 1863-1944
The sick girl 1896
etching and drypoint
13.7 x 17.7cm
Purchased 1987

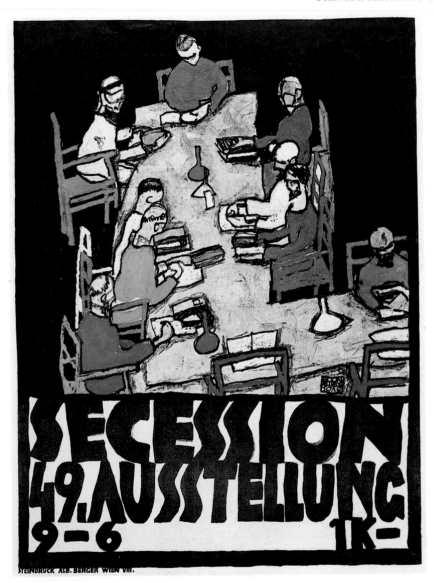

STEINDRUCK ALB. BERGER WIEN VIII.

Kokoschka (1886-1980), Emil Nolde (1867-1956), Käthe Kollwitz (1867-1945) and Rolf Nesch (1893-1975).

European art from the Renaissance to the romantic era is chiefly represented by engravings, etchings and other prints. The beginnings of a serious collection were made in the late 1930s when the Gallery voted money for the London adviser Harold Wright to buy a group of engravings, etchings and woodcuts by European masters of the past. His purchases included good examples of Albrecht Dürer (1471-1528), Federico

EGON SCHIELE
Austrian 1890-1918
Poster for the Vienna Secession 49th exhibition 1918
colour lithograph
67.8 x 53.2cm
Purchased 1979

Barocci (1526 or *c*.1535-1612), Rembrandt (1606-69), van Ostade (1610-85), van Dyck (1599-1641), Wenzel Hollar (1607-41) and Canaletto (1697-1768). Three major Rembrandt etchings were bought in 1948 on his advice, to add to this initial group; the monumental *Christ presented to the people*, 1655 (illus.) has remained the outstanding work of art in the Gallery's collection.

The nucleus established by Harold Wright was increased by the bequest received in 1939 from Sir Philip Street, a former Chairman of Trustees at the Gallery. It then remained relatively static in subsequent years, but over the last decade some serious attempts have been made to broaden the scope of the collection with judicious purchases of works by such artists as Goltzius (1558-1616), Salvator Rosa (1615-73), Giovanni Battista Tiepolo (1696-1770) and Francisco Goya (1746-1828). It is still a small collection, but with some works of real distinction and a certain strength in showing the late Renaissance and Mannerist movements and the seventeenth century, particularly in the

REMBRANDT VAN RIJN
Dutch 1606-69
Christ presented to the people (1655)
drypoint 35.5 x 45.2cm
Purchased 1948

FRANCISCO
GOYA Y LUCIENTES
Spanish 1746-1828
The sleep of reason produces
monsters 1799
etching and aquatint
21.5 x 15cm
Purchased 1978

Netherlands at the time of Rembrandt, but also in France and Italy.

The British landscape tradition which had such a strong part in the development of Australian art is represented by an important collection of the *Liber Studiorum* by J. M. W. Turner (1775-1851), mezzotints by John Constable (1776-1837) and etchings by Thomas Girtin (1775-1802). Their visionary contemporary William Blake (1757-1827) is shown by his engravings for the *Book of Job, 1825* (illus.). Later British prints include some pre-Raphaelite works, a good group of etchings by James McNeill Whistler (1834-1903) — which were to have such a strong influence on the development of etching in Australia — and a series of later British etchings of the 1920s.

With a certain French bias tempering the predominantly English emphasis of the collection from its beginnings, the Gallery has pursued a policy of building up a rich and varied series of French graphic works of the nineteenth and twentieth centuries. A

small group of engraved portraits from the beginning
of the last century contrast in their formality with the
new development of lithography and the rise of
Romanticism, particularly the work of the leading
master Eugène Delacroix (1798-1863). This part of the
collection is still small. The etching revival of the 1850s
and 1860s is more fully represented. The brooding
solitary genius of Charles Meryon (1821-68) in his
Eaux-Fortes sur Paris and his New Zealand scenes is
of special interest. The artist, who visited Sydney briefly

WILLIAM BLAKE
British 1757-1827
Illustration to the Book of
Job (1825)
engraving
21.9 x 16.9cm
Purchased 1949

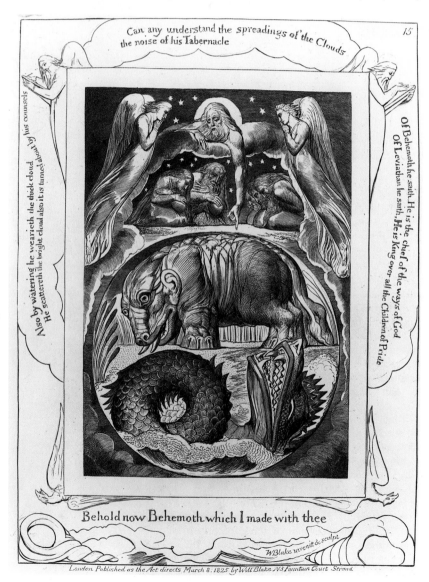

Can any understand the spreadings of the Clouds
the noise of his Tabernacle

15

Also by watering he wearieth the thick cloud
He scattereth the bright cloud also is turned about by his counsels

Of Behemoth he saith, He is the chief of the ways of God
Of Leviathan he saith, He is King over all the Children of Pride

Behold now Behemoth which I made with thee

W Blake invenit & sculpt

London Published as the Act directs March 8, 1825 by Will Blake N3 Fountain Court Strand

when a sailor in the 1840s, was to die virtually unknown, yet his work had a powerful influence on succeeding generations. A group bought for the National Gallery of Victoria in 1891 inspired the pioneers of etching in Australia, John Shirlow (1869-1936) and the younger Lionel Lindsay, and two of the etchings in the collection originally belonged to Lindsay.

Renewed experimentation in lithography from the mid-1860s gradually led to the innovative use of colour lithography and the posters of the 1890s, notably by

PIERRE BONNARD
French 1867-1949
La Revue Blanche 1894
colour lithograph
80.9 x 62.5cm
Purchased 1978

Henri de Toulouse-Lautrec (1864-1901), Pierre Bonnard (1867-1947) and Edouard Vuillard (1869-1940). Recently a further sixty posters for opera and theatre, ranging in date from Jules Chéret (1836-1932) in 1868 to Maurice Dufrène (1876-?) in 1930 has been added to this part of the collection.

The early twentieth-century masters Henri Matisse (1868-1954) and Pablo Picasso (1881-1973) are each represented by several works, including a powerful fauve woodcut by the former and a cubist still life by the latter, as well as plates from the Vollard suite.

A small number of drawings enriches this part of the collection: J. J. Tissot's (1836-1902) *Two studies of a woman* is one of the boldest and most attractive of these, and complements the oil painting and the etchings by the same artist in the collection. Probably intended as a study for a painting which was not eventually carried out, Tissot's young woman charmingly invokes the costume and the atmosphere of France in a leisurely mood.

The development of etching in Australia in the 1890s had a precursor in the amateur E. L. Montefiore (1820-1894) who was exhibiting etchings from 1866 and into the 1870s; he was to be one of the founders of this

HENRI MATISSE
French 1869-1954
Three-quarter length nude with arms raised (1906)
woodcut 34.2 x 26.5cm
Gift of the Art Gallery Society of New South Wales 1976

Gallery and its first Director from 1892 to his death in 1894. The Gallery began to buy original etchings from Europe — Whistler, Tissot and D. Y. Cameron (1865-1945) — and these would have had some influence on local practitioners. Etching was taken up initially in Melbourne by John Shirlow, followed by Lionel and Norman Lindsay and others; soon it was also being attempted, independently, in Sydney by the artists Livingston Hopkins (1846-1927) and Julian Ashton (1851-1942). Its peak of popularity came in the 1920s and into the 1930s, and is quite well represented. Of note is an extensive collection of the work of Sydney Long (1871-1955).

One of the most agreeable and interesting movements in the history of Australian art is the development in the 1920s and 1930s of woodcuts and linocuts. Lionel Lindsay (1874-1961) and Napier Waller (1894-1972) were among the first to exhibit their prints in 1923; by the late 1920s Margaret Preston (1875-1963) had established herself as one of the most prominent exhibitors of woodcuts in Sydney and brought great energy and originality to the medium. Her most striking work *Wheel flower* was bought for this collection in 1929, the year in which it was first exhibited; since then the Gallery's holdings of her work

E. L. MONTEFIORE
Australian 1820-94
Pigeon Bay Creek, Banks Peninsula, N.Z. (1868)
etching
14.9 x 24.9cm
Gift of Jane Macgowan 1985

ERIC THAKE
Australian   1904-82

An Opera House in every
home   1972
linocut
13.7 x 21.2cm
Gift of Hal Missingham 1973

KEN WHISSON
Australian   born 1927

Man seated   1967
drawing; pen and black ink

Purchased 1984

have been increased by gifts and purchases. The Department also holds Japanese woodblock books which once belonged to her, and on which she drew for inspiration.

Preston's contemporary Thea Proctor was also prominent in the Sydney art world and her bold and decorative woodcuts with their luminous hand-colouring are also treasures of this part of the collection. The inventive activity of the period is widely represented by other artists, including pupils of Thea Proctor, and also three artists who studied at the Grosvenor School of Art in London and returned to Australia to show dynamically modern colour linocuts — Ethel Spowers (1890-1947), Dorrit Black (1891-1951) and Evelyn Syme (1888-1961).

Artists who continued the tradition into the 1940s and 1950s and beyond, notably Eric Thake (1904-82), Noel Counihan (1918-86) and Weaver Hawkins (1893-1977), can be compared with a younger generation who revitalized printmaking at the beginning of the 1960s, particularly Henry Salkauskas (1925-79) and Sue Buckley (1911-86) in Sydney and Tate Adams (born

MARGARET PRESTON
Australian 1875-1963
Gum blossom c.1928
woodcut; hand-coloured
27.3 x 26.3cm
Purchased 1964

REDBACK GRAPHIX
(Michael Callaghan,
Gregor Cullen)
Australian, formed 1979
What now Mr Mao 1979
colour screenprint
77.4 x 49.6cm
Purchased 1983

1922) in Melbourne. Over the past fifteen years the collection of Australian woodcuts and linocuts has been greatly increased and now ranges from the early experiments of Blamire Young (1862-1935) and Violet Teague (1872-1951) to recent woodcuts by John Nixon (born 1949) and Vivienne Littlejohn (born 1948).

An interesting aspect of the 1970s is the poster movement, using screenprinted posters to make widely disseminated social and political statements. The first important group was the Earthworks Poster Collective, disbanded eight years ago; their contribution has been continued by another co-operative, Redback Graphix.

Photography

In 1975 the family of the eminent Australian pictorialist photographer Harold Cazneaux (1878-1953) generously donated ninety of his finest images to the Gallery. This gift inaugurated the photographic collection and logically directed the first highly selective acquisition policy implemented in 1976. The goal of this policy was to survey Australian 'art' photography from the turn of the century to the 1960s. During the first two years the major emphasis for acquisitions was placed on Australian pictorial photography (1890-1940). The Australian practitioners of this style, Cazneaux's main contemporaries and fellow members of the 'Sydney Camera Circle' (1916-38), had consciously followed the English pictorialist trend away from factual photographs and towards evocative impressionistic 'interpretations'.

From its earliest years photography had followed a contentious path towards recognition and acceptance as an art form. Debates on the medium continually raged in the form of 'photography versus art'. By 1892 however a new issue entered the debate and factionalized the photographers themselves. The push of the

HAROLD CAZNEAUX
Australian 1878-1953

Silver and Grey, Circular Quay pre 1914
bromide photograph
16 x 16.2cm

Gift of the Cazneaux family 1979

JOHN KAUFFMANN
Australian 1868-1942
Turkey 1910-20
carbon print, circular image
diam 29cm
Gift of Mr John Bilney 1978

1880s to make photography more accessible and 'so simple a child could do it' swelled the amateur 'snapshooter' ranks and played a part in the development of the first real art movement in photography — Pictorialism.

The photographers split into two camps — those who advocated the romantic soft focused pigment prints typical of the pictorialist and those who argued that these 'fuzzy wuzzy' photographers only imitated other print mediums and denied the capabilities unique to photography. It was the pictorialist work that proved more popular. The style continued to grow in popularity worldwide, dominated the salon exhibitions and peaked in popularity between 1924-26. Pictorialism arrived later in Australia and lasted longer.

It has been suggested that John Kauffmann (1865-1942) who studied photography in England and Europe introduced the style to Australia. Kauffmann on his return to Adelaide in 1897 joined the South Australian Photographic Society and regularly exhibited his delicate impressionistic images. His work met with praise from the critics and general public alike. The general trend towards Impressionism and the specific qualities of Pictorialism are evident in *Turkey*, c.1910–20, (illus.) one of his finest images acquired by the Gallery in 1978.

The Gallery had established an excellent Australian pictorialist collection by 1978 with the Cazneaux gift providing the nucleus for the holding of Australian and European pictorialist work. Harold Cazneaux was inspired by the work of John Kauffmann and the South Australian pictorialists. From the beginning his imagery had a distinctive style and he progressively treated non-pictorial subjects in the romantic pictoralist manner as in *Silver and grey*, pre 1914, (illus.). This image is an excellent example of Cazneaux's vision, skill and versatility.

Although the photography gallery did not open until 1982, a number of photographic exhibitions were displayed from 1975 onwards. Cazneaux's work was exhibited in 1975 and his images of Sydney made from 1904 to the 1930s were displayed in 1978. In 1979 the first exhibition largely drawn from the Gallery's own collection, 'Australian Pictorial Photography' 1898-1938, was displayed.

With the ambitions of the first stage of the acquisitions policy largely realized the emphasis was placed on the period and style that immediately followed Pictorialism — that of 'modern' photography. As the popularity of Pictorialism waned in Europe a new movement developed, initially in the Weimar Republic (1927-33), and quickly spread worldwide. Just as photographic realism had been challenged by Pictorialism, Pictorialism was to be challenged by those of the new school who championed abstraction and objectivity. The style reached Australia through advertising, publications and photography magazines. Max Dupain (born 1911) was the young, influential Australian photographer who was to pursue the modern cause.

Dupain became interested in photography and joined the New South Wales Photographic Society while still at school. He began working in the commercial studio of the prominent pictorialist Cecil Bostock (1884-1939) in 1930. He formed the 'Contemporary Camera Groupe' in 1938 and was joined by the more progressive pictorialists Cazneaux and Bostock. He passionately advocated a break from pictorialist values and was to strive for the 'modern' cause with its characteristic clean lines, strong light and impersonal geometric forms. *The sunbaker*, 1937, (illus.), with its taut formality and modernist energy

MAX DUPAIN
Australian born 1911
Sunbaker 1937
silver gelatin photograph
38.3 x 43.8cm
Purchased 1976

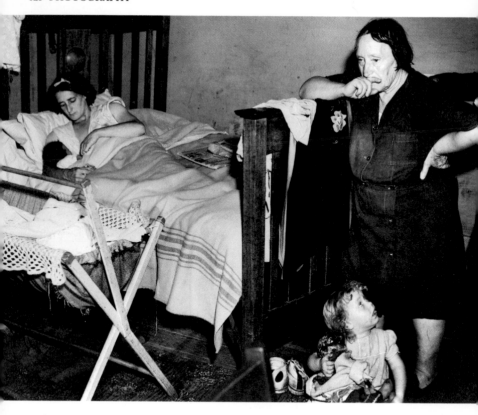

is one of Dupain's most well known and respected images.

Dupain was one of the major figures in Australian photography in the 1930s and 1940s and indeed remains so today. The Gallery placed special emphasis on acquiring a body of his work and displayed this in the Max Dupain retrospective held in 1981. Photographs by Dupain's significant peers including Hal Missingham (born 1906), Athol Shmith (born 1914), Laurence le Guay (born 1917) and his pupil David Moore (born 1927) were also acquired.

David Moore began working in Max Dupain's studio in 1948. His interest in documentary photography quite logically extended to his later work as a photojournalist in the 1950s. *Redfern interior*, 1949, (illus.) is typical of the superb work he produced for the portfolio entitled 'Sydney at Mid-Century' when only twenty-two. Forty works from this period were donated by the Art Gallery Society in 1985, enhancing the fine holdings of Moore's work.

A thorough representation of works by the pioneers of Australian modern photography was largely realized by 1979. However the representation is continually strengthened with significant acquisitions, like the Hans Hansenpflug (1907-77) Collection donated by the artist's son in 1984.

Since its inception the Photography Department has adhered to formal policies emphasizing specific styles and particular periods. The traditional bias has been towards Australian work. However these restrictions also resulted in many valuable areas of photography being neglected, specifically contemporary, nineteenth-century and international works. Subsequent policies have sought to balance the collection and rectify the earlier omissions. From 1979 contemporary Australian photography was highlighted as an area worthy of special attention. Such acquisitions were selected from both the traditional or 'straight' photographic mode and those part of the hybrid photographic forms and manipulated imagery of the 1970s.

Contemporary Australian photography in its myriad of forms now constitutes a major part of the collection.

ROBYN STACEY
Australian born 1952
Father and child 1983
hand coloured silver gelatin photograph
33.6 x 41.5cm
Purchased 1984

GRANT MUDFORD
Australian born 1944
Port Waratah from conveyor
tower 1981
silver gelatin photograph
46.5 x 57.7cm
From the CSR Photography
Project Collection
donated 1987

It remains an active area of acquisition and the recently donated CSR Collection containing three hundred and fifty works by twenty-four photographers has done much to enhance this area of the collection. Expatriate photographer Grant Mudford (born 1944) has applied his formal clear vision to the commission with great success (illus.).

Further support for the Australian contemporary collection has come from Hallmark Cards of Australia and Anne Ferran's (born 1949) work from her series entitled *Scenes on the death of nature* 1986, (illus.), is just one of the works added to the collection through their support.

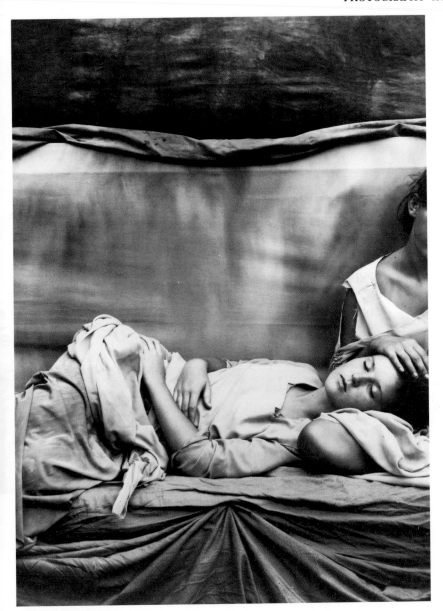

ANNE FERRAN
Australian   born 1949

Scenes on the death of nature,
IV   1986
silver gelatin photograph
154 x 115cm

Purchased 1987 Hallmark
Cards Photographic Collection
of Australia

From 1984 a concentrated emphasis has been placed on building up a collection of Australian nineteenth-century work, a previously neglected area. The Gallery now has an excellent selection of works by renowned nineteenth-century photographers including Charles Bayliss (1850-97), (illus.) Nicholas Caire (1837-1918) and J. W. Lindt (1845-1926) (illus.).

International works are represented, of necessity, on a more selective basis. From the outset it was recognized as a mistake to see Australian photography in isolation and out of a broader context — equally it was realized that the rarity and cost of international works obviously posed significant problems. The solution to this dilemma was two-fold: it was decided to concentrate on acquiring a small but worthwhile collection of works that enhanced the texture of the Australian collection, and to involve the Gallery in tours of photographic exhibitions from other collections both within Australia and overseas.

The international collection now holds seminal works by influential non-Australian photographers from both the nineteenth and twentieth centuries. These photographers include P. A. Emerson (1856-1936), Julia Margaret Cameron (1815-79) and Bill

CHARLES BAYLISS
Australian 1850-97
Shearing shed *c.*1890-7
albumen photograph
15.2 x 20cm
Purchased 1984

J. W. LINDT
German/Australian 1845-1926
Mullawirraburka (King John)
Kaiwina Tribe (Coorong)
albumen photograph
17.3 x 13.1cm
Purchased 1984

BRASSAI (GYULA HALAZ)
Transylvanian/French
1899-1984
Filles de Montmartre 1932
silver gelatin photograph
39.3 x 29.1cm
Purchased 1986

Brandt (1904-83). The international works by Eugene Atget (1856-1927), Brassai (1899-1984) (illus.) and Man Ray (1890-1976) (illus.) point not only to the merit of the individual photographers, but also serve to highlight the growing strength of the international collection as a whole.

MAN RAY
American/French   1890-1976
Solarized portrait   late   1920s
silver gelatin photograph.
28.5 x 22.2cm

Purchased 1987

View of the Australian
collections in the old wings
with Bertram MacKennal's *The
dancer* (1904) in the
foreground.

Information

Hours

The Art Gallery of New South Wales is open Monday to Saturday from 10.00am until 5.00pm; Sunday from 12 noon to 5.00pm.

The Gallery is closed on Christmas Day and on Good Friday.

(For selected special exhibitions the Gallery opens at 10.00am on Sunday.)

Tours

Free guided tours are presented by the Gallery's Volunteer Guides and leave from the entrance foyer at the following times:

Monday 1.00pm and 2.00pm; Tuesday to Friday 11.00am, 12 noon, 1.00pm and 2.00pm; Saturday and Sunday 1.00pm, 2.00pm and 3.00pm. Special theme tours leave each Wednesday at 12.30pm on a topic which is advised in the Gallery's weekly advertisement in the *Sydney Morning Herald*. Bookings for special tours can be made by telephoning the Education Office on (02) 224 1740.

The Gallery Shop

The Gallery's main bookshop is located to the left of the entrance foyer and is open from 10.00am to 5.00pm. Another sales point is located on level 3 adjacent to the coffee shop. The Gallery Shop carries the largest range of art books in Australia, which reflects not only the Gallery's collection but other subject areas as well. Postcards, greeting cards, prints and posters of images from the collection, and gift items such as replicas, are also stocked.

Members of the Gallery Society, schools and libraries, receive a 10% discount. For telephone enquiries call the Gallery Shop direct on (02) 225 1718.

The Gallery Restaurant and Café

The Gallery Restaurant is located on level 5 and has a fully comprehensive menu. Reservations can be made by telephoning (02) 232 5425.

The café is located on level 3 and serves light meals and sandwiches.

Both restaurant and café are open from 10.00am until 4.30pm.

Photography
Visitors are permitted to take photographs for their personal use only after completing a permission form available from the information desk. Tripods and open flashbulbs are not permitted. Only works from the permanent collections can be photographed; requests for commercial photography must be addressed to the Director in writing.

The Art Gallery of New South Wales Foundation
The Art Gallery of New South Wales Foundation was established as a Trust in 1982 to raise a Capital Fund, the interest from which is to be used by the Trustees to acquire major works of art.

The New South Wales Government has promised to match, on a dollar-for-dollar basis, contributions from the private sector up to a limit of $4 million, thus creating a potential capital base of $8 million.

All donations to the Foundation of $2 or more are tax deductible. Enquiries should be directed to the Secretary of the Foundation on (02) 225 1752.

Special Benefactors

Art Gallery Society of New South Wales
Mr and Mrs J. K. Bain
Bond Street City Freeholds Ltd.
Sydney Cooper
The Estate of the late Mervyn Horton
Katies Ltd.
Ken Myer

Foundation Membership

Membership of the Art Gallery of New South Wales Foundation is divided into four categories. The category of membership is determined by the level of contribution to the Foundation over a five year period.

Founder Benefactors
Art Gallery Society of New South Wales
Government of the State of New South Wales
Mr C. Lloyd Jones
News Limited

Governors
Amatil Ltd.
Ampol Exploration Ltd.
Ampol Ltd.
ANZ Banking Group Ltd.
Australian Consolidated Press Ltd.
The Australian Gas Light Company
Boral Ltd.
BP Australia Ltd.
Caltex Australia Ltd.
Castlemaine Tooheys Ltd.
CSR Ltd.
Esso Australia Ltd.
FAI Insurances Ltd.
Goodman Fielder Ltd.
The late M.E.R. Horton
James Hardie Industries Ltd.
Lend Lease Corporation Ltd.
Lotto Management Services Pty. Ltd.
Mr G.E. Mapp
National Australia Bank Ltd.
Rothmans of Pall Mall (Australia) Ltd.
The Shell Company of Australia Ltd.
Thomas Nationwide Transport Ltd.
Westpac Banking Corporation
and one anonymous

Fellows
The late Sir Howard & Lady Beale
Blue Circle Southern Cement Ltd.
Brambles Industries Ltd.
Brenmoss Group Holdings Pty. Ltd.
Mrs E. Capon
G.J. Coles & Coy. Ltd.
Commonwealth Banking Corporation
Commonwealth Industrial Gases Ltd.
Costain Australia Ltd.
C.R.A. Services Ltd.
Davids Holdings Pty. Ltd.
Mr J.O. Fairfax
Mr & Mrs P.A. Flick
Mr S.M. Gazal
George Patterson Pty. Ltd.
Mr M.A. Gleeson-White
Mrs M. Gowing
Mr & Mrs S.D.L. Horwitz
ICI Australia Ltd.
John Fairfax Ltd.
Mrs V.N. Kahlbetzer
Mrs R. Komon
Mayne Nickless Ltd.
McCann-Erickson Advertising Pty. Ltd.
Mr R. Rivkin
Mr & Mrs P.G. Saywell
State Bank of New South Wales
Mr & Mrs E. Sternberg
St. George Building Society
Mr G.M. Thorp
Unilever (Australia) Ltd.
Utah Foundation
Mr & Mrs P. Weiss
Mr R. Whyte
Woolworths Ltd.
and one anonymous

Ordinary Members
Mr J. Abercromby
Mr Ross Adamson
Albert Investments Pty. Ltd.
Mr & Mrs T.R. Allen
Allied Mills Ltd.
Mr W.P. Anderson
Amalgamated Wireless (Australasia) Ltd.
The late Mrs I.M. Ashton
Australian Guarantee Corporation Ltd.
BAG Holdings Pty. Ltd.
Barclays Bank Australia Ltd.
Broken Hill Proprietory Company Ltd.
Mr A.D. Bishop
Mrs B. Bishop
Mrs M.R. Bleasel
Bond Street City Freehold
Mrs N. Brink
Mrs G. Bunning

Mr M.D.I. Burrows
Mr P.H. Cary
Ms N. Cash
Mr & Mrs D. Clarke
Concrete Constructions Pty. Ltd.
Mr D.N. Constable
Dr. M. Coppleson
Mr J.N. Creer
Mrs R. Danziger
Mrs V. Davies
Dawson Waldron
Mr G.M. Douglass
Edward Lumley Ltd.
Ernst and Whinney
Mr & Mrs E.A. Floyd
Foundation Madelon
Mr B.C. France
Dr. and Mrs J. Friend
Mr M. Galloway
George Weston Foods Ltd.
Mr N.H. Grace
Mr E. Graf
Mr & Mrs J. Grant
The Greater Union Organisation
Ms G. Green
Mr & Mrs N. Gruzman
Mr B.A. Guy
Mr & Mrs I.R.L. Harper
Mrs R.G. Hartwig
Mr W.P. Hartwig
Mr & Mrs A.G. Hatsatouris
C.E. Heath Underwriting & Insurance (Aust.)
Pty. Ltd.
Mr & Mrs. S.R.N. Heath
Honeywell Limited
Mrs M.T. Hooke
Sir Leslie Hooker Memorial Foundation
Mr B.C. Hudson
Hungerford Hill Wines Pty. Ltd.
Hunt & Hunt
Dr. & Mrs J. Indyk
Japan Chamber of Commerce and Industry,
Sydney
Japanese Society of Sydney
Mrs G.O. Jennings
The Hon. Sir Asher Joel, KBE
John Clemenger NSW Pty. Ltd.
Mr & Mrs R.H. Kidd
Kimberly-Clark Australia Pty. Ltd.
Mrs J. King
The James N. Kirby Foundation
Mr A.G. Leggie
Leo Buring Pty. Ltd.
Mr & Mrs J.D. Lewis
Ms C. Liddy
Lindemans Wines Pty. Ltd.
Lintas Pty. Ltd.

Mr I. Macarthur Onslow
Mr F.I. Markovic
Miss Y.D.B. May
McConnel Smith and Johnson Pty. Ltd.
Mr & Mrs R.P. Meagher
Ms J. Meek
Mercantile Credits Ltd.
Mercedes-Benz NSW Pty. Ltd.
Mrs John Minter
Mr R.H. Minter
Mojo — MDA
Monier Limited
Morgan Stanley International Inc.
The late Mrs J. Muston
Mr S.B. Myer
Mr J.H. Myrtle
National Panasonic (Aust.) Pty. Ltd.
Ord Minnett
Mr J.D. O'Toole
P. & O. Australia Ltd.
Lady Florence Packer
Pan Continental Mining Ltd.
Partnership Pacific Ltd.
Mr J.H. Pascoe
Pechiney Australia Pty. Ltd.
Peko-Wallsend Ltd.
Phillip Cox & Partners Pty. Ltd.
Mr Brent Potts
Dr. & Mrs G.C. Potts
Lady Potter
Reader's Digest Services Pty. Ltd.
The late Mrs W.M. Redhead
Dr. L. Rees
Rouge Homme Wines Pty. Ltd.
Mr & Mrs M.T. Sandow
Mr T.K. Schrecker
Sedgwick Pty. Ltd.
Mrs P. Seidler
Miss R.A. Smith
Mr & Mrs N. Sparnon
Thorn EMI (Australia) Ltd.
Transfield Pty. Ltd.
Vincent Fairfax Family Trust
Mrs F.G.D. Voss
The Hon. Mr Justice T.W. Waddell
Mrs D. Walder
Mr L. Walford
Wattyl Limited
J.B. Were and Son Charitable Fund
Mr & Mrs J. West
Westgarth Baldick
Willis Faber Johnson & Higgins Pty.
Ltd.
Mr D. Wolanski
Mr & Mrs K. Woolley
Wormald International Ltd.
Mrs C. Zampatti

Art Gallery Society

Founded in 1953 by a small group of art lovers who felt the Gallery would benefit from the support of an independent membership organization, the Art Gallery Society has become the Gallery's most important link with the wider community and an invaluable fund raising resource. From a modest few hundred enthusiasts thirty five years ago, the Society has grown to over 20,000 members who enjoy a special relationship with the Gallery and who receive many benefits not available to the casual visitor.

The Society was set up with twin aims; to help the Gallery reach out and involve the community and to assist in the development of the Gallery's collections. The Society's success in pursuing these objectives has seen a steady growth in membership to a point where it is now the largest organization of its type in Australia and an impressive list of important works of art join the collections through Society funding.

With its large and growing membership the Society has been able to marshall considerable financial resources to help the Gallery develop its collections. It has done this primarily by funding the purchase of works which the Gallery may not have otherwise been in a position to buy.

Its first purchase was in 1959 when it bought a Godfrey Miller oil, 'Nude and the Moon'. Since then, 25 works have joined the collection through funds provided by the Society, an astonishing array of art covering painting, sculpture, drawing and photography. Notable amongst the works credited to the Society are Frank Stella's giant canvas *Khurasan gate,* George Lambert's *Holiday in Essex,* a Chinese Tang dynasty equestrian figure *c.*AD700, and a Henry Matisse lithograph *Nude with arms raised.*

The Society has also supported the Art Gallery Foundation, and, with gifts totalling $250,000, the Society is the largest non-government donor to this important fund.

The Gallery's valuable ON SIGHT mobile art service was partially funded by the Society as were a large number of the unique 'Australian Eye' series of films. This series was a Society initiative which resulted in Film Australia producing 30 films on important Australian paintings.

Another aspect of the Society's work is the Volunteer Guides service, a group of dedicated Society members who provide guided tours for the public, school children and VIPs. The 100 volunteer guides undergo a training programme in which they study art history, Australian art and the Gallery's collections in depth, and attend special lectures on visiting shows. Their prodigious knowledge of the Gallery is available to any casual visitor and each year they guide up to 30,000 people through the collections.

A second volunteer group, the Task Force, also operates under the Society's auspices. This group provides a valuable resource to enable the Gallery to mount many visiting exhibitions. The Task Force provides Society members with a more active involvement with their Gallery, one that allows them to participate in its operation rather than being merely a spectator.

At the core of the Society's activities is its events programme which presents over 120 functions each year. Films, lectures, private viewings, music, dance, local and overseas tours, plus special events for young people and families are offered to satisfy the experienced art lover and the newcomer alike. The events programme gives members a behind the scenes look at the Gallery, the opportunity to hear and meet artists, and the chance to be part of the development of the Gallery.

Members have their own space in the Gallery, an elegant and comfortable set of rooms well equipped with a comprehensive library, facilities for drinks and with audio visual arts material.

Members receive a monthly arts magazine which keeps them up to date on new exhibitions at the Gallery and news of the wider world of art. The Gallery also extends many concessions to members such as discounts at the Gallery shop, reduced admission charges to major exhibitions and free previews of visiting shows. Also available is a reciprocal rights scheme that provides travelling members with similar benefits at galleries and museums interstate and overseas.

The underlying theme of the Society is to help make the Gallery more accessible to the community. It is the link which helps visitors take away from the Gallery more than simply an impression of what they have seen and of the institution which houses the works they have enjoyed.

Membership of the Art Gallery Society

Information about joining the Society and the benefits of membership may be obtained by telephoning 225 1742 or visiting the Society's rooms on level 1 of the Gallery.

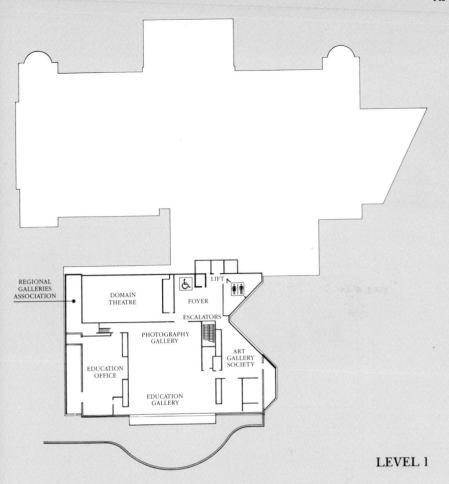

REGIONAL
GALLERIES
ASSOCIATION

DOMAIN
THEATRE

FOYER

LIFT

ESCALATORS

PHOTOGRAPHY
GALLERY

ART
GALLERY
SOCIETY

EDUCATION
OFFICE

EDUCATION
GALLERY

LEVEL 1

An Education Officer taking a
tour.

144

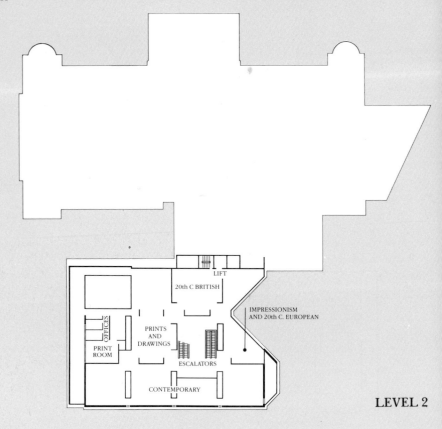

LEVEL 2

View of the 1987 Perspecta
exhibition.

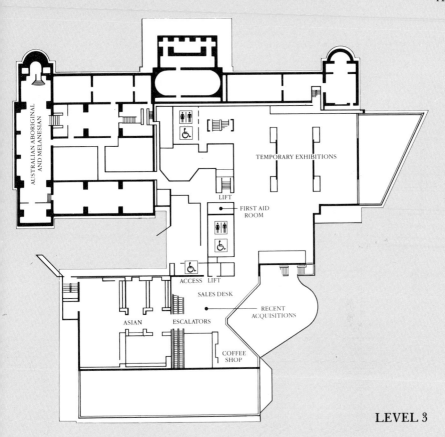

AUSTRALIAN ABORIGINAL
AND MELANESIAN

TEMPORARY EXHIBITIONS

LIFT

FIRST AID
ROOM

ACCESS LIFT

SALES DESK

RECENT
ACQUISITIONS

ASIAN   ESCALATORS

COFFEE
SHOP

LEVEL 3

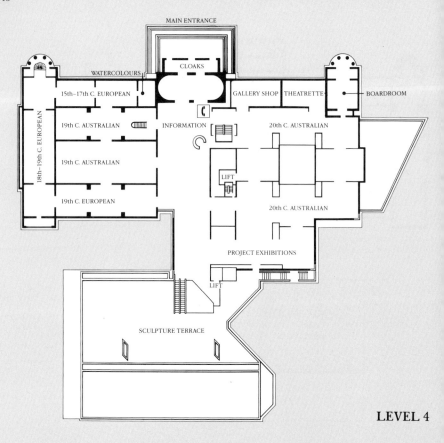

MAIN ENTRANCE

CLOAKS

WATERCOLOURS

15th–17th C. EUROPEAN

18th–19th C. EUROPEAN

19th C. AUSTRALIAN

INFORMATION

19th C. AUSTRALIAN

19th C. EUROPEAN

GALLERY SHOP   THEATRETTE   BOARDROOM

20th C. AUSTRALIAN

LIFT

20th C. AUSTRALIAN

PROJECT EXHIBITIONS

LIFT

SCULPTURE TERRACE

LEVEL 4

View of the European
collections in the old wings
with John Gibson's *Hunter
and dog* (1860s) on the right.

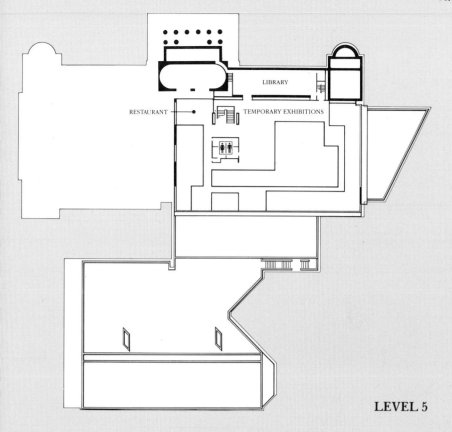

RESTAURANT

LIBRARY

TEMPORARY EXHIBITIONS

LEVEL 5

Gallery restaurant.